W9-CLS-440

SLEIGHT OF HAND

SLEIGHT OF HAND

106 AMAZING CARD & COIN TRICKS

Bob Longe,
Sheila Ann Barry,
William A. Moss,
Alfred Sheinwold,
David Knowles,
Charles Barry Townsend

Main Street
A division of Sterling Publishing Co., Inc.
New York

2 4 6 8 10 9 7 5 3 1

Published by Sterling Publishing Co., Inc.
387 Park Avenue South, New York, NY 10016

Material in this book previously appeared in
The Little Giant ® Book of Card Tricks © 2000 by Bob Longe,
Classic Card Games & Tricks © 2002 by Sheila Anne Barry, Bob
Longe, William A. Moss & Alfred Sheinwold, *Classic Magic Tricks*
© 2002 by Bob Longe, David Knowles, and Charles Barry
Townsend, *The Little Giant ® Book of Magic Tricks* © 2002 by
Bob Longe, *Card Tricks Galore* © 1999 by Bob Longe, *Clever
Card Tricks for the Hopelessly Clumsy* © 2000 by Bob Longe

© 2003 Sterling Publishing Co., Inc.

Distributed in Canada by Sterling Publishing
c/o Canadian Manda Group, One Atlantic Avenue, Suite 105
Toronto, Ontario, Canada M6K 3E7
Distributed in Great Britain by Chrysalis Books
64 Brewery Road, London N7 9NT, England
Distributed in Australia by Capricorn Link (Australia) Pty. Ltd.
P.O. Box 704, Windsor, NSW 2756, Australia

ISBN 1-4027-1110-7

Contents

CARD TRICKS

Controls: sleight tips

As I grow older and older, it becomes increasingly difficult to astonish me. Still, I am astonished at how many young magicians have no idea of how to control a card—that is, to bring a selected card to the top or bottom of the deck. Certainly, many tricks do not require it, but a person planning to perform a variety of card tricks should learn at least one good card control, and should be able to perform it effortlessly.

Here are four you might want to try out. The first three of these are of my own invention; the other is a standard method of controlling a card. I have found that all of them are quite effective.

A Card Above

In this one, the chosen card may be brought either to the top or the bottom. Let's assume you want to bring the card to the top. A spectator chooses a card. You fan through the deck for its return. The spectator places his selection among the cards. You make sure the chosen card is atop the unfanned pile in the left hand, while the remaining cards remain fanned in the right hand. The two sections are not actually separated, as you can see in Illus. 1.

CHOSEN CARD

Illus. 1

THESE TILTED DOWN
TO THE RIGHT

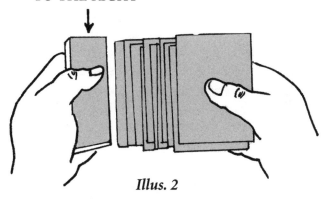

Illus. 2

As you proceed, try not to stare at your hands. The eyes of the spectators tend to follow your eyes, so content yourself with a casual glance. And, at the key moment when you're closing up the cards, try not to look at all.

Tilt the cards in your left hand slightly clockwise (Illus. 2). At the same time, close up the cards in your

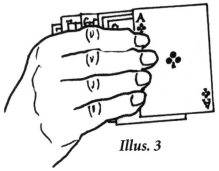

Illus. 3

right hand against the left thumb. As you do this, with your right fingers push to the left the bottom card of those in your right hand. Illus. 3 shows the view from below without showing the pile in the left hand.

Continue closing the fan, letting this bottom card fall on top of the cards in the left hand. With your right hand, lift off all the other cards you closed up. On top of the cards in the left hand is an indifferent card, followed by the chosen card.

With your left thumb, push off the top card of those in your left hand (Illus. 4). As you do, say, "It should go in about here."

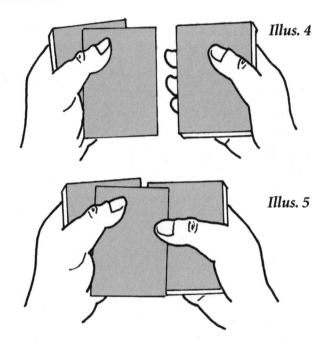

Illus. 4

Illus. 5

With your right thumb, pull it onto the top of those in your right hand (Illus. 5). Place the cards in your left hand on top of all. The chosen card is now on top of the deck. Spectators believe that it is buried in the middle of the deck.

(With magicians, I sometimes say, "I prefer to transfer the card so that I know the card above it." They realize that the presumed chosen card now has the original bottom card above it in the deck.)

Suppose you want to bring the chosen card to the bottom of the deck. You apparently perform the exact same routine: fanning through the cards; closing up the cards so that the top card of those in the left hand is the one chosen; placing this card on top of the pile held in the right hand; and placing the remaining cards in your left hand on top.

Actually, before you close up the fanned cards, you push the chosen card a bit to the right with your left thumb and tilt the cards in your left hand slightly clockwise. This makes it easy for you to add the chosen card to the bottom of the group in the right hand. Separate the hands slightly. As before, push off the top card of those in the left hand, add it to the top of those in the right hand, and put the remaining cards from the left hand on top of those in the right hand. The chosen card is now on the bottom of the deck.

A Little Extra

I'm very proud of this one, which is also quite effective. In fact, I've even fooled magicians with it. The key is to perform the necessary moves casually, but smartly.

Illus. 6

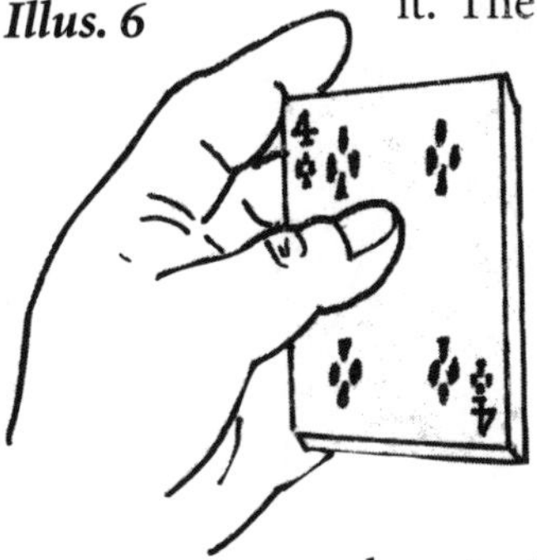

A card is chosen. You fan through the deck for its return. When the spectator replaces the card, you put one more card on top of it. As you slide the fanned cards onto the pile in the left hand, insert the tip of the left little finger, holding a break. (See pages 69 to 71.) Even up the cards with your right hand, still retaining the break.

The situation: You're holding the deck in the dealing position in your left hand, with the left little finger holding a break one card above the chosen card. The right hand grips the deck from above, fingers at the outer end, thumb at the inner end.

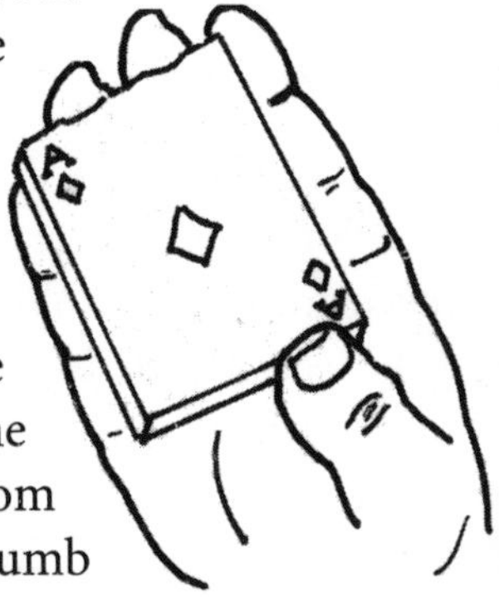

Illus. 7

As soon as the cards are evened up, lift off all the cards above the break with the right hand. Turn the right hand palm up, turning that packet face up. At precisely the same time, place the left thumb under the other packet and turn it face up, also Illus. 6 and 7 shows the position at this point.

Illus. 8

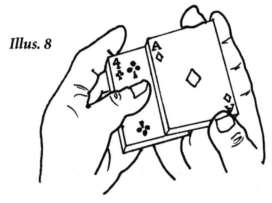

Place the cards that are in the right hand on top of those in the left hand (Illus. 8). Close up the cards and even them up. You're now holding the deck precisely as you were just before you turned the two piles over; the only difference is that the deck is face up.

Fan out several cards at the face of the deck, showing them. At the same time, say, "Obviously, your card is not on the bottom . . ."

Fan out several middle cards, saying, " . . . but some-where in the middle."

Close up the deck and turn it face down. Turn over the top card, remarking, "And, of course, it's not on top."

The chosen card is now at your disposal, second from the top.

Try this one out. It's actually quite easy. I think you'll like it.

By the way, it's easy enough to get the card to the top, if you want it there. Chat for a moment with the group, lying about what you propose to do. Turn the deck over. "As you can see, your card isn't on the bottom." Place the bottom card into the middle. Turn the deck face down again. Show the top card and place it into the middle, saying, "And your card isn't on top."

Here's another way: Casually give the cards an over-hand shuffle. At the beginning, draw off the top two cards individually. This brings the chosen card to second from the bottom. Give the cards another over-hand shuffle. With the first move, squeeze your left thumb and fingers together, drawing off both the top and bottom cards. As you finish the shuffle, draw off the last few cards separately. The chosen card is on top.

The Double-Cut

This excellent sleight is actually a complete cut of the deck. Suppose you want to bring a selected card to the top of the deck. Have a card chosen. Fan the cards from hand to hand for the return of the selection. The spectator sticks the card into the deck. As you close up the deck, slightly lift the cards above the chosen card with

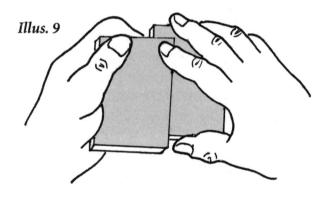

Illus. 9

the fingers of the right hand. This enables you to get a break with your left little finger above the chosen card. (See pages 69 to 71.)

By the way, if you plan to bring the selection to the bottom, get a break below it.

Holding the deck from above in the palm-down right hand, transfer the break to the right thumb. With the left hand, take from the bottom about half the cards below the break and place them on top. You must raise your right first finger a bit to allow passage of the cards.

With the left hand, take the rest of the cards below the break and place them on top (Illus. 9).

Notes:

(1) This basic sleight is useful in a variety of ways in many tricks.

(2) The sleight is probably even more deceptive if you move three small packets from below the break instead of two.

Simplicity Itself

In some instances, this control works best. For example, you might want to bring the chosen card to a fairly high number from the top. This would do perfectly, as I'll explain.

Before the spectator chooses a card, sneak a peek at the bottom card of the deck. You can do this as you separate the deck in two, preparing to do a riffle shuffle (Illus. 10). Then, when you shuffle, keep the card on the bottom. Easier yet, look at the bottom card as you tap the side of the deck on the table, apparently evening up the cards (Illus. 11).

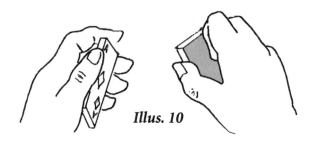

Illus. 10

So you know the bottom card of the deck. Fan out the deck, and a spectator selects a card. Close up the deck. From the top of the deck, lift off a small packet and drop it onto the table. Lift off another small packet and drop it on top of the first one. After dropping several packets like this, say to the spectator, "Put your card here whenever you want." After you drop one of your packets, he places his card on top. You put the rest of the deck on top of it. Even up the cards and pick them up. The card that you peeked at is now above the chosen card.

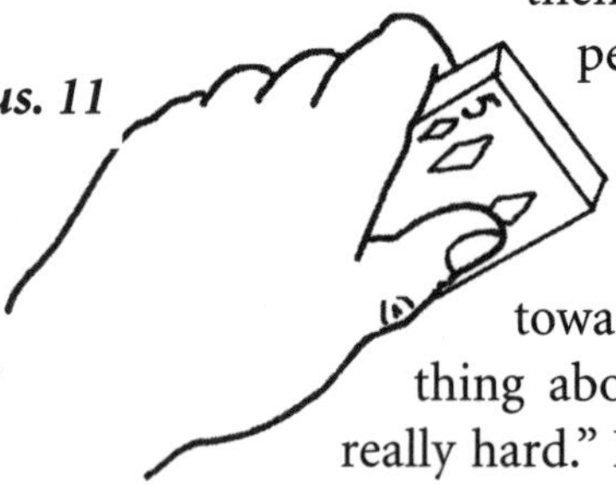

Illus. 11

Start fanning through the cards, their faces toward yourself. Mutter something about, "This is going to be really hard." Fan off several cards. Cut them to the rear of the deck. Fan off several

more. Again, cut them to the rear. You're establishing a pattern so that it won't seem so odd when you finally cut the chosen card to a key position.

Let's say you simply want the card available on top of the deck. Continue fanning groups of cards and placing them at the rear until you see that you'll soon arrive at the key card. The card on the near side of the key card is the one chosen by the spectator (Illus. 12). Cut the cards so that the key card becomes the top card of the deck (Illus. 13). Just below it, of course, is the chosen card. Turn the deck face down.

"I can't seem to find your card." Turn over the top card of the deck (the key card). "This isn't it, is it?" No. Turn the card over and stick it into the middle of the deck. Turn the deck face up. "How about this one?" No. Take the bottom card and stick it into the middle of the

Illus. 13

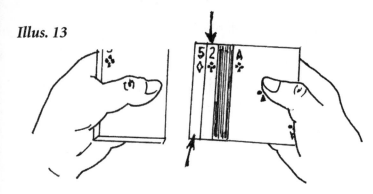

deck. Turn the deck face down. The chosen card is at your disposal on top of the deck.

Suppose, for purposes of a specific trick, you want the chosen card to be 10th from the top. Again you start by fanning off small groups and cutting them to the rear of the deck. When you get to the chosen card, you start counting to yourself. You count the chosen card as "One." Count the next card as "Two." Cut the cards so that the card at "Ten" becomes the top card. The chosen card is now 10th from the top.

Controls: tricks

Sneaky Slide

Have a card chosen and bring it to the top of the deck. (See Double-Cut, page 18.) Double-lift the top two, showing the wrong card. Turn the double card face down on top. "There you are, five of clubs," you declare. But the spectator says that you're wrong. You replay: "Oh-oh! I guess I'll have to try real magic."

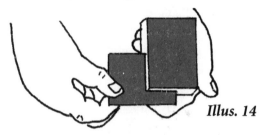

Illus. 14

Take the top card off the deck, grasping its outer edge with your right hand. Pass it through the middle of the deck, from the front end to the back. Turn the card over, showing that it has magically changed to the chosen one.

My Mistake

Have Elizabeth choose a card and show it around. When she returns it to the deck, bring it to second from the top. Simply obtain a little-finger break *one card above* the chosen card after it's returned. Then perform a double-cut (see Double-Cut, page 18).

Explain to the group, "I know you're going to be astonished by this effect, but please hold your applause. When I reveal the chosen card, just marvel in silence so that we all can enjoy the enormous impact."

Perform a double-lift, showing the selected card. Name the card, and then say, "Oh, I'm sorry. I really don't miss that often. I have no idea what went wrong."

Return the double card to the top of the deck and slide the top card into the middle of the deck.

"Maybe I can work something out." Ask Elizabeth, "What was the name of your card?"

She tells you the name. All the spectators will be happy to inform you that you just stuck the chosen card into the middle of the deck.

"That's all right," you say. "After all, I *am* supposed to be a magician."

Tap the top card and turn it over.

That's Right, You're Wrong!

I developed an improved handling of a trick called "Righting a Wrong," which appeared in Jean Hugard and Fred Braue's *The Royal Road to Card Magic*.

Ask Barney to choose a card. When he returns it,

bring it to the top. (See Double-Cut, page 18.) "Barney," you say, "please think of any number from 5 to 15."

Hand him the deck and ask him to count off that number onto the table. Ask him to *look at* the last card dealt.

"Is that your card?" No. Have him replace the pile on top. "I don't like to criticize, but maybe you didn't count them exactly right."

Pick up the deck. Suppose his chosen number was 11. Deal off ten cards slowly and precisely. "The important thing is to deal the cards *slowly*. Now wouldn't it be amazing if I had your card right here? What was your card?"

Suppose Barney says, "Queen of spades." You double-lift the top two, showing, say, the ten of clubs. "Oh, no, the ten of clubs. I should have guessed. The ten of clubs is a real troublemaker, always popping up when you least want it."

Turn the two face down, and deal the top card (the one chosen) face down onto the table to one side. "So we'll just eliminate that nasty ten of clubs." Place the dealt cards back on top of the deck, commenting, "The trouble is, I dealt the cards *too slowly*. If you deal the cards too slowly, this will never work."

Count off ten cards onto the table, saying, "Now it should work." Show the top card. It's the ten of clubs. "Ten of clubs again! Wait a minute . . . What was your card again?" Turn over the card on the table. "That's it!" Act disgusted. "Just what I thought. The ten of clubs ruined everything."

One in Four

Remove from the deck the four, three, two, and ace of any suit. (Let's assume that you're using diamonds.) First find the four and place it face up on the table. On top of this, place the face-up three, followed by the two and the ace.

Ask Jeannine to choose a card and show it around. When she returns it to the deck, bring it on the top. (See Double-Cut, page 18.)

Hold the deck in the dealing position in your left hand. Pick up the four face-up cards from the table and drop them face up on top of the deck. Spread them out, along with another card or two. Say, "Here we have the ace, two, three, and four of diamonds." As you close up the four of diamonds with your palm-up right hand, get a break with your left little finger below the fifth card. Immediately, turn your right hand palm down and lift off the packet of five cards, fingers at the outer end,

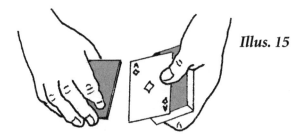

thumb at the inner end. The top, face-up card of the packet is the ace of diamonds, followed by the other three diamonds in order. On the bottom of the packet is the face-down chosen card.

"It's important that you remember the order of the cards," you say. "First, we have the ace." You now turn over the ace lengthwise and add it to the bottom of the packet. Here's precisely how: Move the packet in your right hand over the deck and hold down the ace with your left thumb as you move the rest of the packet to the right, drawing off the ace. The ace should extend over the right side of the deck about half its width (Illus. 15). From below, lift the packet in your right hand so that its left edge flips the ace over sideways. *Leave your left thumb in place, so that the ace falls on it.* Bring your left hand over the face-down ace, so that the ace is added to the bottom of the packet.

Call attention to the two of diamonds, saying, "And here we have the two." In the same way as you did the ace, turn the two of diamonds face down and add it to the bottom of the packet.

In exactly the same way, show the three and then the four. Drop the packet on top of the deck.

On top of the deck is the chosen card, followed by the ace, two, three, and four of diamonds.

Say to Jeannine, "I'd like you to choose one of the four cards—ace, two, three, or four. In fact, think of one, and then change your mind. I want you to have complete freedom of choice." She chooses one of the cards.

Suppose the ace is chosen. Deal the top card face down onto the table, saying, "All right, there's the ace. Now let's see how the two behaves." Without showing the top card, place it second from the top. Tap the top card and then turn it over. Apparently the two has returned to the top. Place the two *face up* next to the card on the table.

"Let's check the three." Place the top card second from the top. Tap the top card and turn it over. The three has returned. Deal it face up next to the two.

"And the four?" Again, place the top card second from the top. Tap the top card and turn it over, showing that the four has returned. Deal it face up to the right of the three.

Gesture toward the table. "So we have ace, two, three, and four of diamonds. And you chose the ace. What's the name of your card?" The spectator names it. Turn over the face-down card. Success!

Suppose the spectator chooses two, three, or four. In each instance, the chosen number is simply dealt face down onto the table; each of the others is placed second from the top, brought back to the top, turned face up, and dealt face up onto the table.

Let's suppose Jeannine chooses three, for instance. "Fine," you say. "Let's see how the ace behaves." Place the top card second from the top. Tap the top card, showing that the ace has returned. Place the ace on the table face up.

Place the top card second from the top, saying, "Let's see what the two does." Tap the top card. Sure enough, the two has returned to the top. Deal it face up to the right of the ace. Deal the next card face down to the right of the other two cards, saying. "Here's your three."

Once more place the top card second from the top, saying, "Let's see what the four does." Tap the top card; the four has returned to the top. Deal it face up to the right of the other three cards.

In all instances, you finally ask the name of the chosen card and then turn it face up.

Jacks Be Nimble

Start by taking the jack of hearts and the jack of spades from the deck and tossing them face up on the table. "Here we have the one-eyed jacks, and they have most peculiar properties, as you will see."

Remove a card from the deck and, without showing its face, place it on top of one of the face-up jacks, and place the other face-up jack on top of both. Explain: "Place a card between the jacks, and what do we have? Right. A one-eyed-jack sandwich."

Spread the deck for the selection of a card. Tell the spectator to look at his card and set it down for a moment. Pick up the jack sandwich and place it on top of the deck, saying, "Let's get rid of the jack sandwich." Give the cards a complete cut.

"Yes, we really do have the jack sandwich in the middle." Fan through the cards to show the jack sandwich. As you close up the deck, obtain a break below the uppermost jack with the little finger of your left hand. Transfer the break to your right thumb and perform The Double-Cut (see page 18).

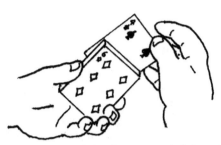

Illus. 16. Hold the deck high in your left hand at the tips of fingers and thumb, and carefully draw the card away from you.

You now have a face-up jack on the bottom, an indifferent card face down on top, and a face-up jack second from the top. Place the deck on top of the spectator's card, saying, "Did everyone see the selected card? No?"

Pick up the deck and turn it over, holding it face up in your left hand. As you display the chosen card, name it. "Now," you say to your volunteer, "I want you to pick the exact point at which I should cut the deck."

This is where you get rid of that extra card on top, the one nearest your left palm. Tilt the deck downward and then carefully draw the card away with your right hand. Your best bet is to hold the deck high in your left hand at the tips of fingers and thumb, and carefully draw the card *away from* you (Illus. 16). Hand it to the spectator. "Stick it partway into the deck, anywhere you want."

Wherever he sticks the card, meticulously cut the face-up cards so that his inserted card becomes the card on the face of the deck. Straighten up the cards and set the deck on the table face down.

"In the deck we have your chosen card and jack sandwich. Let's take a look and see if the card in the jack sandwich can tell us anything about your card."

Fan through the face-down cards and remove the jack sandwich. Turn it over, showing the selected card between the jacks. "See how smart I was? I picked *your* card to put into the jack sandwich."

Note: This trick is quite similar to the previous trick in its basic principle. But its effect is quite different. Roy Walton combined tricks by Al Baker and Dai Vernon; my only contribution is to add a slightly different handling.

The "Milking" Trick

Turn your back and ask a spectator to quietly deal two piles of cards with the same number in each pile. He can have, say, ten to twenty cards in each pile. "Set the rest of the deck aside," you say. "We won't be using it. Now look at the top card of one of the piles and remember it. Pick up the other pile. Take a smaller number of cards from that pile and place them on top of your chosen card. Hide the pile you're holding."

Turn around and pick up the packet containing the spectator's card. "We must give the packet a mystical double-card shuffle," you explain. Grip the cards from above with the left hand, thumb at the inner end, fingers at the outer end. Begin "milking" the cards into a single pile. That is, remove a card from the top and bottom at the same time with the thumb and fingers of the right hand and drop them into a pile (Illus. 17). Continue until all the cards are dealt this way. If one card remains, place it on top.

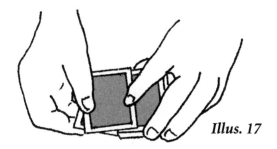

Illus. 17

Illus. 17 *Remove a card from the top and bottom at the same time with the thumb and fingers of the right hand and drop them into a pile.*

Pick up the pile and toss out the bottom and top cards face up. "Neither of these is your card, right?" You are right. Place both cards face down on top of the packet. You have managed to add an additional card to the top of the packet.

Point out that you have no way of knowing how many cards the spectator has concealed. Ask him to take these cards and deal them into a pile as you deal yours into a separate pile. You deal card-for-card from your packet as he deals his cards. When he deals his last card, turn over the card you are dealing. It is the chosen card.

Note: This is a modification of a trick invented by Alex Elmsley and revised by Stewart Judah.

Good Choice

Here's a fast, clever trick requiring only nerve and a bit of practice.

In your pocket, you have four kings. The king of spades and the king of clubs have blue backs. The king of hearts and the king of diamonds have red backs. The order doesn't matter.

Remove the four cards from your pocket, making sure spectators cannot see any of the backs. Hold them face up in your left hand. Spread the kings out and ask Ted to name one (Illus. 18). After he does so, say, "You can change your mind if you want to, Ted—it doesn't matter." When he finally decides on one, remove it from the group, saying, "This one." Replace it so it's the lower-most of the face-up cards. Maneuver the other cards about so the king of the same color as the one chosen is at the face of the packet. As you do this, say, "You could have chosen this one, or this one, whatever one you wished." Tell him that he can still change his mind. If he does, maneuver the cards so they're in the appropriate position described.

You are about to perform a variation of the *flushtration count*, the invention of Brother John Hamman. Close up the face-up packet and hold it from above in your right hand, fingers at the outer end and thumb at the inner end. Turn your right hand palm up, displaying the back of the top, chosen card. Let's assume Ted has selected the king of clubs. Say, "It's amazing that you should choose the king of clubs, which has a *blue* back." Turn your right hand palm down. With the left *fingers*, draw the king of clubs from the back of the packet into your left hand. (This first maneuver differs from the standard *flushtration count*.) Turn your right hand palm down and, with your left thumb, draw off the card at the face of the packet so that it comes to rest on top of the king of clubs. (This is the standard move in the *flushtration count*.) Perform the action again. Then display the back of the last card, turn your right hand palm down

and drop the card face up on top of those in your left hand.

Ted has chosen the only card with a different-colored back.

Further Thoughts: *If you wish, repeat the trick several times. Simply put the cards into your pocket. Chat for a moment about what a coincidence has occurred. Then say, "I have another set of kings in my pocket." Dig into a different pocket. "No luck. Maybe they're here." Take the same set of kings from your pocket and repeat the trick. You might even put the kings away again and then go through the same routine. The basic trick is so deceptive that there's little danger that spectators will catch on, and it becomes quite amusing when spectators suspect that you're using the same kings.*

Let's Play Jacks

In a "sandwich" trick, a chosen card is discovered between two significant cards, usually jacks. "Sandwich" tricks are always colorful and fun. This version by Al Leech is not only easy, but also extremely effective. I have revised the basic move slightly to make the trick even easier.

Take the red jacks from the deck and place them onto the table face up. Say, "The red jacks are real buddies. Generally, they like being together all the time. I'll try to prove that in a minute. But first, let's have Charles choose a card."

Charles selects a card. When he returns it to the deck, get a little-finger break above it. (See When a Card is Returned, pages 69 to 70.) Bring it to the top of the deck, using The Double-Cut, page 18.

Hold the deck in position to perform an overhand shuffle, but with the faces of the cards toward the left thumb (Illus. 19). Ask Charles to pick up one of the jacks and turn it face down. "Charles, just drop it in here wherever you want. Just tell me when to stop."

Perform an overhand shuffle, taking several cards each time. The cards are landing in your left hand face up. When Charles tells you to stop, do so. Hold out the face-up cards that are in your left hand so that he can place his face-down jack on top. Put the face-up cards that are in your right hand on top of all.

Illus. 19

Turn the deck face down.

"We now have a face-up jack in the deck. I'll show you." Fan down to the face-up jack. Fan past a bit so that you can get a left little-finger break beneath the card below the jack. (This move is identical to that used in When a Card Is Returned, pages 69-70.) You're now holding a little-finger break below the chosen card.

Close up the cards and perform a double-cut, bringing the chosen card to the bottom of the deck.

Have Charles pick up the other red jack. "Turn the jack face up, please. Just tell me when to stop and drop it in."

Turn so that your left side is toward the group. You're about to perform another overhand shuffle, this time with the backs of the cards facing the left thumb, and you want to make sure that no one can see the bottom (chosen) card. As you shuffle this time, the cards land face down in the left hand. Charles

Illus. 20

tells you when to stop and drops the jack *face up* onto the face- down cards in your left hand. You drop the cards that are in your right hand on top of all.

The sneaky part is done.

"I promised that I could bring the red jacks together," you say, which is not quite true. "Let's see how I did."

Fan through the cards until you come to the red jacks with a card in between. "Whoops! What's this!" Take the three from the deck as a group. Make sure they are spread out, so that all can see them clearly as you display them. (Illus. 20). Put the three cards onto the table, still spread out. Set the rest of the deck aside.

Turn to the spectator who selected a card. "It looks as though someone's trying to break up their friendship. What was the name of the card you selected?"

He names the card. You turn over the usurper. Sure enough, that's the card.

Jealousy

How about something old and something new? The plot is old, and my handling is new.

Hand the deck to Matt and ask him to give it a good shuffle. You take the cards back and turn over the top card. "I can't believe what you've done, Matt." Suppose the card is the 3C. "You've shuffled to the top the most jealous card in the deck, the three of clubs. You did a good job, because the three of clubs really likes being on top."

Turn the 3C face down, but in a particular way. Push it off the deck with your left thumb; then grasp it on the outer right corner with the right hand, thumb on top, fingers below (Illus. 21). Turn the card end-for-end, replacing it on the deck face down. This whole procedure enables you to get a little-finger break below the 3C as you put it back onto the deck. (See When Putting Cards on Top of the Deck, page 71.)

You now perform a sleight known as the Braue

Illus. 21

Reversal, named after its inventor, Fred Braue. You're holding the deck in the dealing position in your left hand. Take over the break with your right thumb. (See Transferring the Break to the Right Thumb, page 71.)

You're now primarily holding the deck with the right hand. With the palm-up left hand, take the bottom half of the deck and move it to the left (Illus. 22). Stick your left thumb beneath this packet. Now it's quite easy to flip the packet over, using your left thumb. Place the packet on top of the deck, lifting your right first finger to allow passage. *Continue holding the break with your right thumb.* Naturally, a card is now on view on top of the deck. It's the original bottom card of those you turned over. Let's suppose that it's the AH.

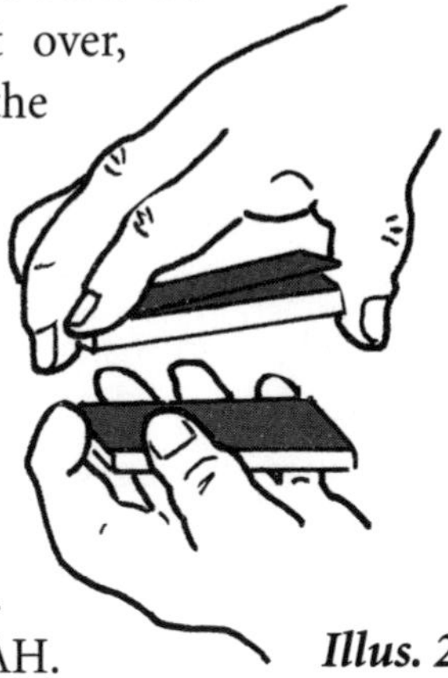

Illus. 22

"The ace of hearts is not a jealous card...not like the three of clubs."

With the left hand, take all the cards *below the break you are holding with your right thumb,* flip these over with your left thumb, and place them face up on top. Another card is now on view at the top of the deck. Let's say that it's the JS. "And the jack of spades doesn't have a jealous bone in his body. No, Matt. The three of clubs is the jealous one."

You're now holding a face-up deck, except for the lowermost card—the face-down 3C.

"And do you know who he's most jealous of? His brother, the three of spades. I'll show you what I mean."

Fan through the face-up cards and find the 3S, take it out, and place it on top of the card on the face of the deck. As you do this, make sure you don't inadvertently show the back of the 3C, which is at the back of the face-up deck.

"Let me demonstrate. "I'm going to treat the 3S in a very special way—so that he'll be faced differently from all the other cards." Lift off the 3S, turn it over, and push it into the deck about a quarter of the way down.

Cut off about half the cards and place them beneath the other half. Turn the deck face down.

"Do you think the three of clubs can stand that? Oh, no, he's extremely jealous." Fan down to the face-up 3S and pull it out of the deck partway. "See, here's the three of spades."

Continue fanning to the 3C and pull it partway from the deck. "And here's his jealous brother. He just *had* to face the same way."

Pause.

"Thank goodness *people* aren't like that."

Note: *At the end of the trick, the face-down cards are spread out somewhat and the two matching face-up cards are sticking out nearly half their length (Illus. 23). This makes quite a striking display; give spectators a chance to see it and enjoy it.*

Magic Locator

Al Smith developed an excellent variation of a well-known principle. The trick has amazing impact when you consider the simplicity of method.

Approach Rob as you fan through the face-down cards. "Just touch a card, please, Rob." When he does so, turn the card face up in place. Name the card. Suppose it's the 7S. "All right, Rob, you chose the seven of spades." Fan through several more cards and get a break with the tip of your left little finger beneath the third card below the face-up card. (This is the same move

involved in When a Card Is Returned, pages 69 to 70.)
As you do this, say, "You might have touched any one of
these cards. Or, in fact, any other card in the deck." This
latter statement you make as you close up the cards.

In our example, you'd now have a face-up seven of spades,
followed by three cards and your inserted little finger.

Casually double-cut the cards so that the face-up card
becomes fourth from the bottom. (See The Double Cut,
page 18.)

Hand the deck to Rob. "Deal the cards into a pile,
Rob." After he has dealt several cards, say, "You can stop
whenever you wish."

He stops. "Please look at the last card dealt and show
it around."

When he's done showing it around, continue, "Put it
back on top of your pile, and put the rest of the deck on
top of it. Finally, give the deck a complete cut."

You talk to the group for a bit, both to build up the
trick and to help the spectators forget precisely what has
happened. So you might say, "I had no way of knowing
what card you'd elect to have turned over. And I could
not have guessed what card you'd choose. But I think
there might be a close relationship between the two
cards. Let's find out."

Holding the cards down so that all can see, you

fan through the face-down deck to the face-up card. Leave the face-up card on top of those in your left hand. Set the rest of the deck aside.

"Let's see if we can spell out the value of this card to find the one you chose."

All the values will spell out with either three, four, or five letters.

Let's say that the value of the face-up card spells out with three letters (ace, two, six, ten). Set aside the face-up card. Pick up the deck and spell out the value of the card, dealing one card onto the table for each letter. Turn over the next card.

If the value spells out with four letters (four, five, nine, jack, king), set aside the face-up card. Pick up the deck and spell out the value, turning over the last card dealt.

If the value spells out with five letters (three, seven, eight, queen), pick up the deck, leaving the face-up card on top. Spell out the value of the card, turning over the last card dealt.

In each instance, ask for the name of the chosen card before turning it over.

One-Card Transposition

My friend Wally Wilson, an extraordinarily versatile magician, passed this trick on to me. It's based on an idea by Al Leach.

Ask Mel to name a number from five to ten. Suppose

he names seven. Count six cards from the top of the deck into a pile on the table. Turn over the seventh card and show it. Let's suppose that it's the QC.

"Can everyone see this queen of clubs?" Everyone can. Leave the card face up as you place it onto the table, a bit to one side.

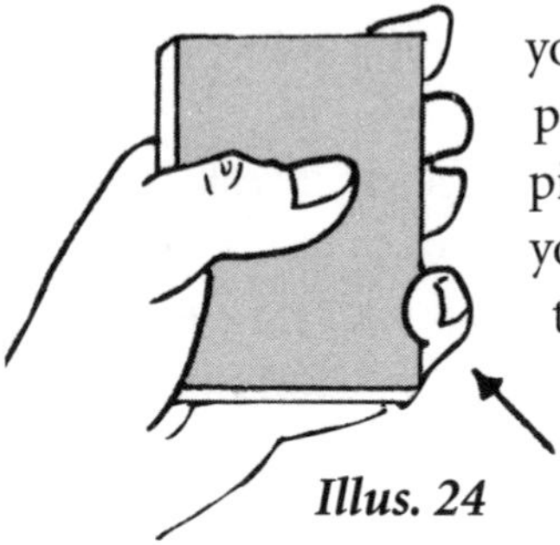

Illus. 24

Pick up the six-card pile with your right hand and prepare to place it on top of the deck. As the pile nears the deck, push the tip of your left little finger against the top of the deck; a portion of the fingertip will project slightly over the deck (Illus. 24). Thus, when you place the six cards on top of the deck, you're holding a left little-finger break beneath them. Transfer the break to your right thumb.

Maintaining the break, take the bottom half of the deck with the palm-up left hand. Slide your left thumb under this packet and flip it over. Put this face-up pile on top of the cards in your right hand. Note that you must raise the right first finger to permit placement of the cards. (This is a variation of "The Double-Cut," page

18.) Also note that you're still holding the break at the rear with your right thumb.

What's the situation? From the top down, the deck is like this: about half the deck face up, six cards face down, a break held by your right thumb, the rest of the cards face down.

With the right hand, move all the cards above the break about halfway off to the right (Illus. 25).

Apparently you have just cut the deck, turning half the cards face up. No one should suspect that you have six face-down cards below the face-up portion.

Hand the face-down half to Mel, saying, "Please look through these cards to make sure we don't have a duplicate queen of clubs."

As he does this, drop your cards on top of the face-up chosen card—in the example, the QC. Pick up the entire pile. Apparently you're holding a face-up pile of cards with the chosen card at the rearmost position. Actually, from the rearmost position on up you have: the face-up chosen card, six face-down cards, and a group of face-up cards.

Now comes the critical part of the trick. As Mel goes through his packet, you must appear to give your cards a casual shuffle. Here's how:

Hold the cards in your left hand in the dealing position, except that your left thumb is against the face of the packet. In other words, you'll be sort of shuffling the cards face up. Draw off the card on the face of the deck with your left thumb. Do this seven more times—eight in all. Drop the rest of the cards on top of (in front of) these eight.

Turn the packet around so that the left thumb is against the back of the packet. Perform exactly the same shuffle, only this time drawing off eight cards from the face-down packet. As before, drop the remaining cards in front of these eight.

The packet is back in its original order.

The entire shuffling procedure should be done casually. Don't look at your hands; instead, watch with great interest as Mel searches for a duplicate QC.

Incidentally, you may add an additional false shuffle if you wish. Turn the packet so that the left thumb is against the face once more. Shuffle off groups of cards as with a regular overhand shuffle. But stop after shuffling off about two-thirds of the packet. Let these cards fall forward toward your left thumb. Drop the remainder of the cards behind these cards. Your top stack remains the same.

Mel has apparently had no luck finding a duplicate QC. "No queen of clubs, Mel?" No. "Hold out your cards face down, please."

He extends his packet face down. Place your group face up on top of his. At this point, Wally suggests that you make a mystical pass over the cards. That's okay with me.

"Please look through the face-up cards and hand me the queen of clubs."

He can't find the queen of clubs among the face-up cards. If he tries to fan through farther, stop him. "Hold it, Mel. Please give me the face-up cards."

He does.

"What number did you choose originally?"

In our example, Mel has chosen the number seven.

"Please count off seven cards from the top of your packet."

He does. And the seventh card-face up and staring him in the face-is the one he chose, the QC.

Card Through Table 1

I believe it was Bill Simon who developed this method of knocking a card through a table. The first requirement is that you must be seated at a table. The second requirement is that you must have a deck of cards.

Have Nancy choose a card and return it to the deck. Bring the selection to the bottom of the deck, using one of the methods suggested in "Controls: sleight tips," pages 10 to 22.

"You could have chosen any one of these cards," you say, fanning through the face-down deck. "I just hope that the one you selected has special qualities, Nancy, because it has an extremely difficult job to do."

Fan right to the bottom, so that when you close the cards up, you can get a break above the bottom card with your left little finger. Transfer this break to your right thumb.

With the palm-down left hand, cut off a pile of cards (Illus. 26). (Notice that the right first finger is raised to allow the packet to be lifted off.) Slap this pile down in the middle of the table. As you do this, the right hand drops slightly below the table. The right thumb loosens its grip, and the chosen card falls into your lap (Illus. 27). Strictly speaking, the card falls on top of your right leg.

As soon as the card is dropped, bring the right hand forward with its pile, placing it on top of the other pile, thus completing the cut.

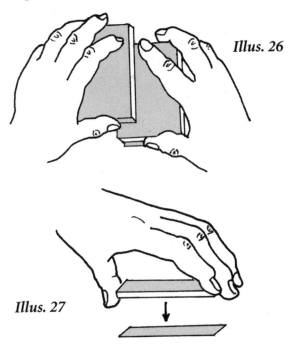

Illus. 26

Illus. 27

The whole business must be smoothly done so that it seems that you have done nothing more than cut the deck.

Display your right hand. "Believe it or not, with this magical hand I can smash the deck on top with such force that it'll bring your chosen card to the bottom. Watch."

Smack the top of the deck with your right hand. Turn the deck over, showing the bottom card. "Is this your card, Nancy?"

Of course not, you silly person.

Try it again. Still failure. "Are you sure?"

She's sure.

"Okay, let me try something. I'll really smack it this time." As you say "really," emphasize the point by holding out both hands, palms to the group.

"Just to be on the safe side . . . " Move your left hand under the table. As it goes under, it grabs the chosen card from your lap and continues to below the position where the deck sits.

Immediately, give the deck a stout smack with your right hand.

"Oh, what's that?"

Slowly bring out the chosen card face down. "Doggone it! I couldn't hit hard enough to knock the card to the bottom; then I go and knock it right through the table. What was the name of your card, Nancy?"

She names it. You turn it over.

Card Through Table 2

This clever refinement of the previous trick is, I believe, the invention of J. Benzais. Again you must be seated at a table. Sitting nearby is Oliver, who always enjoys a good card trick.

Have him select a card and return it to the deck. Bring it to the top, using one of the methods described in "Controls: sleight tips," pages 10 to 22.

Obviously, the card must be put under the table one way or the other. I have added a bit of subtlety to the placement of the card in the lap. You're holding the deck in your left hand. Place both hands on the sides of the chair as you move the chair closer to the table.

After moving the chair in, move your right hand forward to dust off a spot on the table.

Meanwhile, your left hand is palm down, resting on your lap. Naturally, the cards are face up.

As the right hand does its bit of smoothing, thumb off the top card onto your lap. Because your left hand is palm down, the chosen card is the lowermost card, and it lands on your lap face up.

The smoothing with the right hand and the thumbing off with the left hand take place simultaneously.

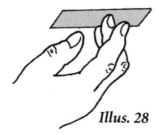

Illus. 28

Illus. 29

Place the deck face up onto the table in the spot that your right hand smoothed.

"Oliver, I'd like you to do something for me." As you say this, gesture toward Oliver with your open hands, showing that they're empty. "Believe me, it's not going to be anything silly or anything difficult."

As you speak, move your right hand below the table level. Pick up the card on your lap and continue the movement under the table to below where the deck rests. With your fingers, push the card face up against the underside of the table (Illus. 28). Push your thumb against the card and remove the fingers from it. Then, as much as possible, turn your hand palm upward (Illus. 29).

As you're doing this, say to Oliver, "I'd like you to reach under the table with your left hand and put it in my hand."

If he puts his hand in yours palm up, fine. If not, with your left hand reach under and turn his hand palm up.

Bring out your left hand.

"Oliver, what's the name of your chosen card?"

He tells you.

"Excellent choice. Now please place your right hand on top of the deck."

He does.

"At the count of three, Oliver, I'd like you to push down really hard on the deck. Ready? One. Two. Three!"

When Oliver starts to push, move your right hand down and away. The chosen card falls into Oliver's hand.

"Oh, you pushed really hard, Oliver. What do you have in your hand?"

He brings his hand out and there, staring at us, is his chosen card.

The Mysterious Spades

British magician Al Smith invented a trick called "Ten Seconds." I changed the handling to eliminate a difficult sleight; I believe that this version is simpler and more direct.

You fan through the face-up deck and toss onto the table the following spades:

A 2 3 4 5 6 7 8 9 10

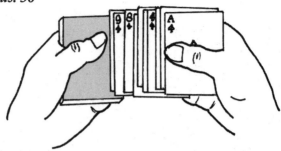

Arrange them in order, so that, as they lay spread out on the table, the lowermost card is the 10S and the uppermost card is the AS.

Tell the group, "I've placed the spades here for two reasons: First, the spades are the cards of mystery; and second, we need ten cards in order."

Leave the ten spades on the table. Have Derek select a card from the rest of the deck. He should look at it, show it around, and then return it to the deck. Bring the card to the top of the deck. (You may use one of the methods described in "Controls: sleight tips," pages 10 to 22, or any other method you like.)

With your right hand, pick up the face-up spades, keeping them somewhat spread out. Place them face up on top of the deck (Illus. 30).

You'll need the help of another spectator. Ilona is very helpful, so say to her, "I'd like you to think of one of these spades—any one you wish." With your palm-up right hand, fan through the spades, going one or two cards beyond.

"Do you have one?"

Ilona says that she does.

Close up the spades, again with the palm-up right hand. As you do this, add an additional card to the bottom of the group. This card, of course, is the one Derek chose.

How exactly do you add this face-down card to the bottom of the group of face-up spades? Your right hand is palm up as you close up the fan of spades. As the cards are closed up, the left little finger gets a break just below the card chosen by Derek. At virtually the same time, turn your right hand palm down and lift off the 11 cards from the deck. With your left hand, set the rest of the deck aside. You're through with it for this trick.

You're now holding in your right hand 11 cards—ten face-up spades and, on the bottom, a face-down card, which is the card Derek selected. Make sure you don't reveal the presence of this extra card.

Address Ilona: "You thought of one of the spades. Which one was it?" She tells you. Let's suppose that she chose the 5S.

Continue holding the pile from above in your right

hand (Illus. 31). With your left thumb, draw off the AS into your left hand (Illus. 32). Using the left edge of the cards in your right hand, pivot the AS face down from below. In other words, the

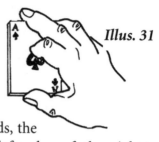

Illus. 31

left edge of the right-hand cards goes beneath the right edge of the AS; the right hand lifts and moves slightly to the left, turning the AS over. As you do this, announce: "The ace of spades."

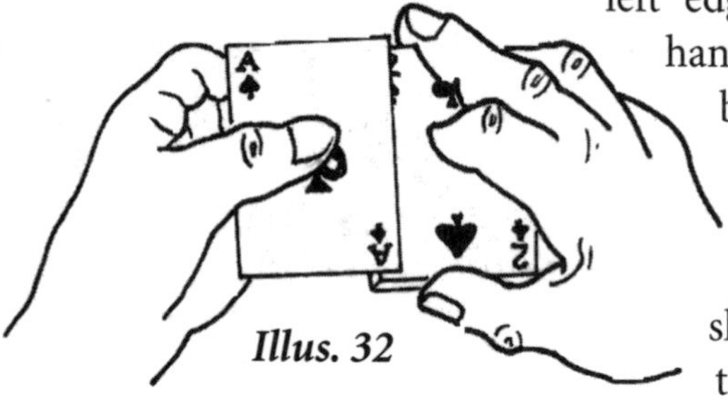

Illus. 32

The group is now looking at the face of the 2S. You name this card and draw it into the left hand with the left thumb. Make sure, however, that it sticks out at least a half-inch to the right of the AS (Illus. 33). Turn the 2S face down on top of the AS in exactly the same way as you turned the AS itself face down.

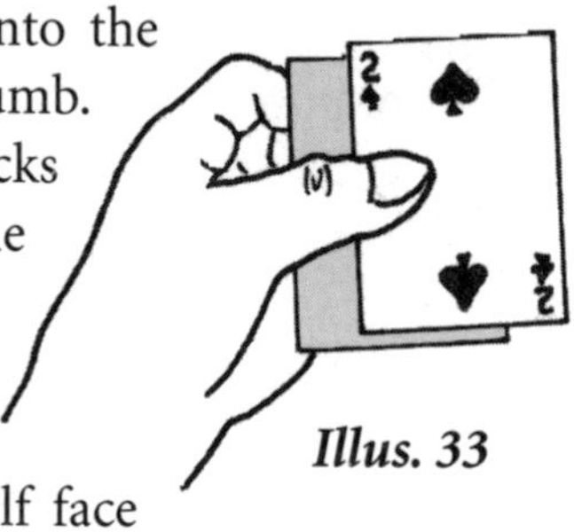

Illus. 33

Continue naming cards, drawing them off, and turning them face down until you come to the card Ilona thought of—the 5S. Draw the 5S onto the cards in your left hand, saying, "And here we have your card, Ilona, the five of spades." Turn it face down, just as you did the other cards. Drop the remaining cards that are in your right hand face up onto the pile in your right hand, saying, "And here we have the rest of the spades." Spread the face-up cards out, showing the remaining spades. With your right hand, lift these face-up spades away and to the right, keeping them spread out. Lower the left hand to the table and thumb off the top card onto the table. Don't say, "And there's the 5S," or anything that specific. Instead, say something like, "There we are."

Turn the cards in your right hand face down and place them on top of those in your left hand.

Pause at this point for a little review. Say to Ilona, "You thought of the five of spades." Casually gesture toward the card on the table.

Say to Derek, "And you selected a card from the deck. So far, no magic at all, right?"

Of course.

"Well, let's see what we have here." In an overlapping row, deal the spades face up from right to left until you come to the chosen number. In this instance, you deal the A to four. Name the cards as you deal them: "Ten, nine, eight, seven, six." Deal the next card face down and protruding toward the spectators an inch or so. As you do, say, "Five." Deal the remaining cards face up, naming the values.

Push the face-down card forward a bit more. "We seem to have an extra five of spades." Pause. "Would any of you be surprised if this turned out to be the chosen card?" Whatever the answer, ask Derek the name of his chosen card. "This can't possibly be it," you say, picking up the protruding card. Turn it over, adding, "This is the five of spades."

Point to the other face-down card. "What's that card there?" Have Derek turn it over. It's his original selection.

Note: When you deal the overlapping row, make sure that you deal from right to left, making an easy-to-read display for the spectators.

Opposites Attract

This wondrous and easy transposition effect is the invention of Roy Walton.

Take from the deck the AS, AH, and the four queens. For the moment, set the four queens aside face up.

Illus. 34

Set the AS face up on the table to the left and, several inches to the right, set the AH, also face up. Cut the remaining deck in two, placing half in front of the AS (away from you) and the other half in front of the AH. Illus. 34 shows this setup from your point of view.

"I'll not insult your intelligence by telling you that the ace of spades is a black card and that the ace of hearts is a red card." Point to each as you say this. "Whoops! Too late."

Pick up the face-up queens and arrange them so that the red queens are at the face of the packet and the black queens are below them. Fan them out and display them face up (Illus. 35). "Again, I won't insult your intelligence by telling you that we have the black queens and the red queens here." Pause. "Darn! Did it again."

You now grip the four queens as

Illus. 35

Illus. 36

follows: Place your left thumb onto the face of the red queen which is second from the face of the fan (Illus. 36). And place your right fingers onto the back of the black queen which is third from the face of the fan (Illus. 37). In this next step, you turn your hands palm down and separate them, apparently taking the red queens into the right hand and the black queens into your left. Actually, as you turn your hands over and inward, you draw into your right hand the red queen on the face of the packet and the black queen, which is third from the face. This leaves a red queen and a black queen in each hand.

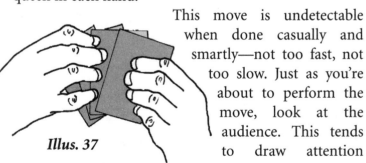

Illus. 37

This move is undetectable when done casually and smartly—not too fast, not too slow. Just as you're about to perform the move, look at the audience. This tends to draw attention away from your hands. As you look at the group, say, "Naturally, the red queens go with the red ace, and the black queens go with the black ace." When you commence the speech, perform the sleight. Set the cards in your right hand face down below (on the near side of) the AH (Illus. 38).

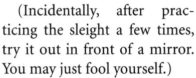

(Incidentally, after practicing the sleight a few times, try it out in front of a mirror. You may just fool yourself.)

Illus. 38

As you can see from Illus. 38, the situation is this: On the table, separated by several inches, are two face-down packets of cards. Below them (nearer to you) are the AS on the left and the AH on the right. Below the AH are two face-down queens, and in your left hand are two face-down queens. In each instance, the top card is a black queen and the bottom one a red queen.

With your right hand, take the queens from your left hand, still keeping them face down. Now take the bottom card (a red queen) into your left hand, leaving the top card (a black queen) in your right hand.

"Naturally, the black queens go with the black ace." Place the red queen (held in the left hand) face down on top of the black ace. It should overlap inward, as in Illus. 39. "And I'll tell you now: The key to this experiment is the ability to make this fancy move when I pick up the ace."

Illus. 39

In a slow, sweeping move-ment, turn the face of the card in your right hand toward the audience (Illus. 40). Then circle your hand a few times before bringing the card down and sliding it face down beneath the AS. Retain your grip on the black queen, for you now lift it and the other two cards and place them on top of the packet which lies in front of them. The audience has had a good look at the face of the queen and subconsciously notices that it's indeed a black queen.

Pick up the packet on which you've just placed the three cards. Spread the cards from the top slightly, saying, "And here we have the temporary home of the black ace and the black queens." Get a little-finger break beneath the ace, which is the second card from the top. Perform a double-cut, bringing the top two cards to the bottom. (See "Double-Cut," page 18.)

Set the packet down to the left. With the right hand, pick up the two face-down queens on the right. "And, it goes without saying that the red queens go with the red ace. So, why did I say it?" Shrug. Take the top card, the black queen, into your left hand and place it on top of the AH. "Now watch as I once more make my magical fancy move." Perform the same sweeping motion as you did previously as you slide the red queen under the AH. The three cards are placed on top of the packet which lies in front of them. Once again, you obtain a break beneath the ace and double-cut the cards. Place the packet down to the right.

Illus. 40

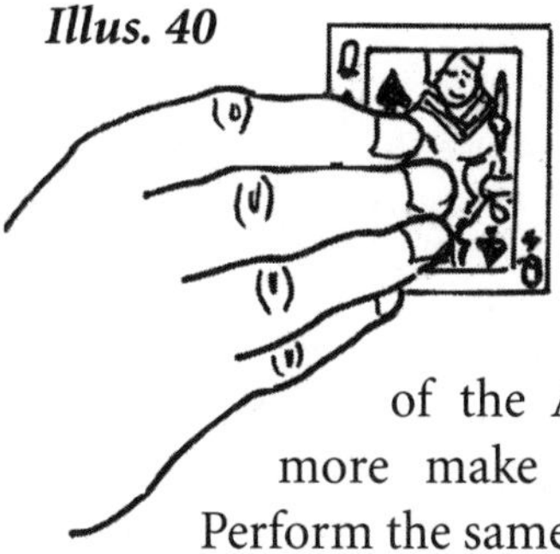

Gesture toward the two packets. Ask, "Which pile should go on top?" Place the indicated packet on top of the other. Cut off about one-quarter to one-third of the cards from the top of the deck. Set this group onto the table, and then complete the cut.

Have a spectator tap the pack. Fan through the cards and take out the first ace you come to along with the card on either side. Set the packet, as is, onto the table. Fan through to the next ace. Again, take it out along with the card on either side. Set this packet onto the table as well.

Turn over the two cards surrounding each ace. The AS now has red queens on either side, and the AH has black queens.

"That just shows that opposites attract."

Notes:

(1) If you read a number of books on magic, you'll eventually come across a comment like this: "Deal the first card face down. On top of it, deal the second card face down, casually letting the audience get a glimpse of its face." No way. Audiences are not so stupid that they don't immediately get the idea that you showed them one card but not the other. So what's my solution? You just read it. Provide a stupid explanation, and then make a big thing out of showing them the card.

(2) Possibly you wondered why I wouldn't want the spectator to put the two piles together and then cut the entire deck. There's simply too much to give away. We certainly don't want the spectators to notice that each pile has a face-up card on the bottom.

False Cuts: sleight tips

An efficient false cut should be done casually, just as a genuine cut would be performed. Often magicians manipulate the cards back and forth between their hands, rapidly shifting piles here and there, and finally end up with a single pile. Naturally, spectators don't know exactly what happened, but they sure as heck know that *something phony was done*. This is not always bad; sometimes it's all right to show that you're skillful. But many of us prefer to keep our skills—however minimal—secret. I recommend this.

Just a Casual Cut

Hold the deck in your left hand. With your right hand, lift off the top portion of the deck and place it face down onto the table. Make some casual remark. At the same time, *without looking at the card*, take the rest of the deck with your right hand. Place this pile *to the right* of those on the table.

Continue commenting. Glance down at the cards on the table. Pick up the pile on the right and place it on top of those on the left. Pick up the combined pile.

The cards retain their original order.

And Another

With the left hand, take the bottom portion of the deck. The left hand should be palm down, and the packet should be grasped with the second finger at the far end, the first finger on top and the thumb at the near end. The top portion of the deck is retained in your right

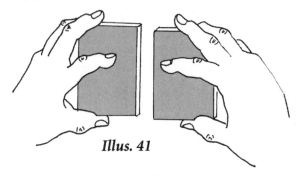

Illus. 41

hand (Illus. 41). Gesture with the left hand as you make a comment. At the same time, drop your right hand somewhat, so that it becomes lower than the left hand.

Place the left-hand portion onto the table. Put the right-hand portion on top of it (Illus. 42). Pick up the entire deck with the right hand.

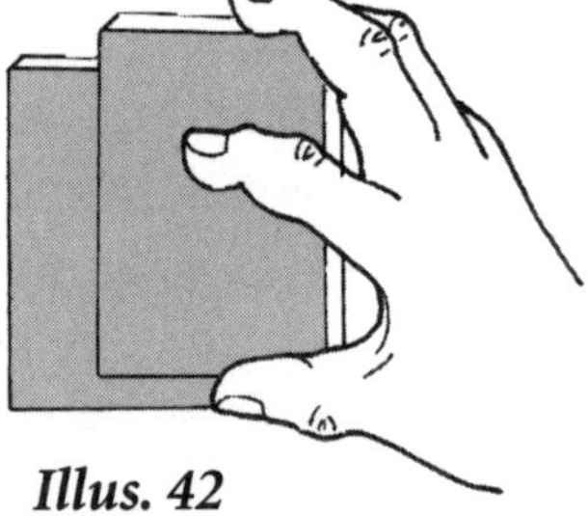

The cards are back in order.

Illus. 42

Give Me a Break

One of the more delicate moves in card magic is obtaining a secret break between cards, either with the left little finger or the right thumb. It's easy enough to do once you understand the concept. Because the secret break is essential to many trick moves, it's not a bad idea to master it.

First, let's consider the little-finger break. Usually, the idea is to obtain only a *small* break and to hold it with only the meaty tip of the little finger (Illus. 43). (In some instances, when doing advanced sleights, the entire first joint of the little finger is inserted.)

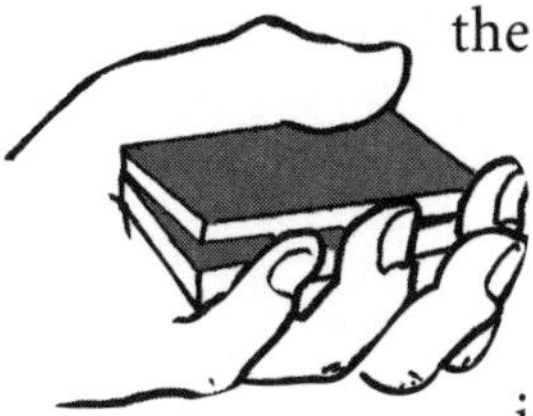

Illus. 43

When a Card Is Returned

How do you obtain this break? It depends on the trick you're doing. Let assume that you're fanning out the cards for the return of a chosen card. Fan cards from your left hand to your right, going through only a small portion at a time, limiting the replacement possibilities. The returned card and all the cards below it should be in a fairly neat pile in your left hand. All the cards above it are held loosely in the right hand. You slightly raise the right side of the cards in your right hand while closing them up. This gives you the opportunity to insert the tip of your left little finger just above the chosen card.

Below the Top Card

Suppose you wish to get a break below the top card of the deck. This can easily be accomplished one-handed. As your right hand is performing some sort of distraction, push the top card slightly off the deck with your left thumb. While drawing it back with the left thumb, insert the tip of your left little finger below it.

Below A Small Number from the Top

Suppose you want to get a break below a small number of cards from the top of the deck—for example, three. Find an excuse to fan out several cards from the top. It could simply be part of the trick you're doing, but, if not, you might say, "You can choose any one of these cards," or, "I can assure you that none of these cards is marked, at least not on this side."

As you fan the cards, let the right fingers rest on the bottom of the third card from the top. Just as when a card is returned, lift these cards slightly at the right side and close up the cards. While doing so, insert the tip of the left little finger below the third card from the top.

When Putting Cards on Top of the Deck
Let's say you're placing three cards on top of the deck, and you'd like to get a break beneath them. It doesn't matter whether you're putting them on top with the hand palm up or palm down. Simply put the tip of the left little finger in position just beforehand (Illus. 44). When the cards are placed on top, the break is taken automatically.

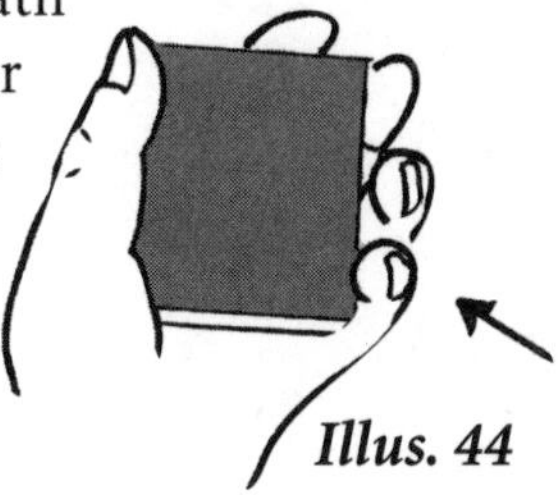

Illus. 44

Transferring the Break to the Right Thumb
In nearly every instance, you'll want to transfer the break to your right thumb. This is almost automatic. Your right hand holds the deck palm down, fingers at the front, thumb at the back (Illus. 45). There is now no need to hold the little-finger break, for your right thumb now has it.

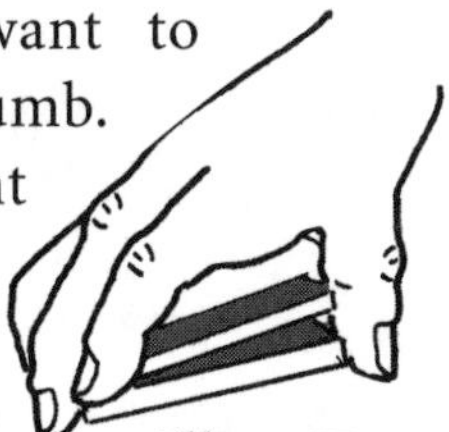

Illus. 45

Table Cut 1

All three of the false cuts in this section are of my own invention.

Hold the packet in the dealing position in your left hand. With your right hand, pick off about the top third of the packet. Place this group in front of you.

Cut off another third with the right hand and place this group forward of the first group.

Take the last third with your right hand and place it forward of the other two groups. Illus. 46 shows the present position.

Pick up the group nearest you and place it on top of the middle group. Pick up the combined packet and place it on top of the farthest group. In that same movement, pick up the entire packet. Place the packet in the dealing position into your left hand.

Illus. 46

Table Cut 2

Again, hold the packet in the dealing position in your left hand. With your right hand, lift off about a third of the cards from the top of the pack, and place this group onto the table.

Cut off another third with the right hand and place it about six to eight inches to the right of the first group.

Take the remaining group with your right hand and place it between the other two piles. Illus. 47 shows the current position.

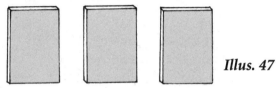

Illus. 47

With your right hand, pick up the pile on the right; at the same time, with your left hand, pick up the pile on the left. Place the group in your right hand on top of the middle pile; immediately place the group in your left hand on top.

Pick up the entire packet with your right hand and place it in the dealing position into your left hand.

Both this and the previous cut should be done fairly rapidly and certainly with no hesitation.

Swing-Around Cut

This rather fancy-looking false cut should be practiced until its performance is second nature.

Hold the deck from above in the right hand, fingers at the front, thumb at the back. Bring the left hand to the deck palm down, so that it is gripping the bottom half of the deck from the side, fingers at the front, thumb at the back (Illus. 48).

Separate the hands. You're holding the top half in your right hand and the bottom half in your left hand. This we will refer to as the Starting Position. Then perform the following moves:

(1) Left hand over right.

Lift the left hand and move it to the right so that the left wrist crosses over the right wrist (Illus. 49). Each hand sets its cards onto the table, but does not let go. The hands are about six inches apart. Each hand is holding about half the deck. Each hand leaves about half its packet on the table and lifts up the remainder.

(2) Left hand over right, coming back.

Now the hands uncross, returning to the Starting Position.

(3) Right hand over left.

The left hand continues to move to the left and then drops down as it swings back to the right, dropping its packet between the two packets on the table. At the same time, the right hand continues its move to the right and then rises slightly as it swings back to the left and passes above the left hand. The cards in the right

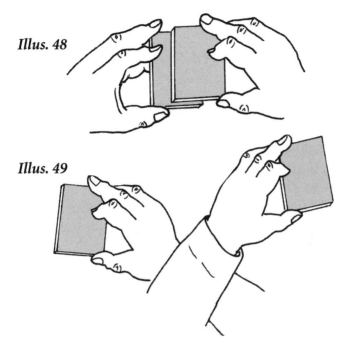

Illus. 48

Illus. 49

hand are then dropped to the left of the other three packets.

The packets are now lined up so that on the far left is the original top portion. To the right of that is the next portion from the top. To its right is the portion that was below that. And finally the lowest portion appears on the far right. In Illus. 50, I have numbered them according to their order from the top.

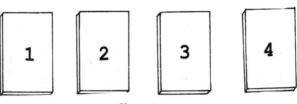

Illus. 50

The packets are then gathered up by taking the packet on the far right with the right hand and sweeping this packet into the left hand. With the right hand, the next packet on the right is swept on top of the packet in the left hand. Then comes the next packet on the right. And finally, the packet which is on the far left. The deck is back in its original order.

You may prefer to gather the cards by placing the packet on the left on top of the packet to its right, the combined packet on top of the next packet on the right, and the combined packet on top of the last packet on the right.

Or, to speed things up, you may pick up the packet on the left with the left hand and the third packet from the left with your right hand. Place each packet on top of the packet on its right. Pick up the combined packet on the left with your left hand and place it on top of the combined packet on the right.

Note: Yes, this cut is rather fancy-looking, but it is completely deceptive, and I have never had anyone question its legitimacy.

Once you've mastered it, you'll find that it's quite easy. The best way to learn the moves is to take from the deck any A, 2, 3, and 4. Place them into a pile, each card standing for a portion of the deck. The top portion is represented by the A, the second by the 2, the third by the 3, and the fourth by the 4. In other words, these are the four packets.

In the initial move, take the bottom two cards with the left hand. Then perform the three basic moves, sweeping the hands as you do.

(1) Sweep the left hand over the right. (Drop the bottom card from each hand.)

(2) Uncross the hands, sweeping the left hand back over the right.

(3) Don't stop but continue the sweeping as you bring the left hand farther left and then under the right, dropping its packet between the other two. At the same time, the right hand continues moving to the right and then sweeps back to the left, crossing over the left hand and dropping its packet to the far left.

False Cuts: tricks

A Cut Above The Rest

Once more the aces are cut, but this time by a *spectator*. This is probably the easiest and most direct of all tricks in which the aces are cut. The only problem is that a sneaky sleight is required. Very few can do the sleight undetectably, so most performers require considerable misdirection. Far better, I figure, to use an easier version of the sleight.

To begin the trick, you must have two aces on top of the deck and two on the bottom. This is easily accomplished in one of two ways: You can start with this trick. Or you can do a four-ace trick earlier in your performance and keep the aces together during ensuing tricks. All you need do, then, is fan through the cards, faces toward yourself, and cut between the aces, bringing two to the bottom and two to the top.

Single out Evelyn. "You look pretty magical to me, Evelyn. How about helping me out."

As you're saying this, you perform the easy sleight I mentioned above.

Turn clockwise about 45 degrees, so that your left side is mostly toward the group. With the left hand, hold the

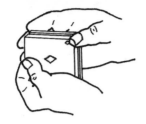

Illus. 51

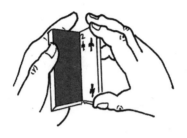

Illus. 52

deck of cards in a variation of the dealing position: The thumb is along the left side of the deck instead of on top, and your left hand is tilted clockwise so that the sides of the deck are parallel to the floor (Illus. 51).

You grip a small group of cards at the top of the deck—ten or so—with your right thumb at the inner end and fingers at the outer end. The grip should be taken on the left side of the cards. You now move the top side of these cards away from the rest of the deck by pivoting the group sideways to the right, as though starting to open the back of a book (Illus. 52).

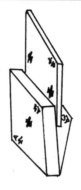

Illus. 53

Your left fingers press against the back of these cards as you pull them up and away from the rest of the deck. The small group clears, but its top card stays as it is pressed against the top of the remaining deck (Illus. 53).

You let the main deck fall so that it is face down in the dealing position in the left hand. Meanwhile, your right hand holds up the small pile you have apparently cut from the top.

(If you choose to do no sleight at all, I have provided a method in the notes at the end.)

The situation: The main deck is face down in your left hand with an ace on top, which you drew from the top of the small packet in your right hand. There are two more aces on the bottom of the main deck. And there is one more ace on top of the small packet you hold in your right hand.

Let everyone see the size of the packet you're holding

in your right hand. "See this packet, Evelyn? I'd like you to cut off a small packet also. It can be a little smaller or a little larger. But don't make it too large, because you're going to have to make three more cuts."

Hold out your left hand so that Evelyn can cut a packet from the main deck. After she takes a packet, have her place it face down onto the table. Compliment her on the quality of her cut. "I don't believe anyone could have cut off a packet any more efficiently than you did, Evelyn."

Meanwhile, you casually place your small packet on top of the cards in your left hand.

"Try it again, Evelyn." Hold out the cards so that she can cut off another packet. This one is also placed face down onto the table.

Two packets are face down on the table, each having an ace on top. There are two aces on the bottom of the deck.

As you compliment Evelyn this time, perform an overhand shuffle. With the first move, you squeeze your left fingers and thumb together, drawing off the top and bottom cards together. In a continuous motion, shuffle off the rest of the cards. When you near the last of the cards, shuffle them singly. The result of the shuffle is that the second card from the bottom (an ace) is on top of the deck and that the bottom card of the deck is still an ace.

Offer the deck for Evelyn to cut off another packet, which she sets face down onto the table. While lavishly praising her technique, you give the deck another overhand shuffle. Again when you near the last few cards, you shuffle them singly, thus bringing the bottom card (an ace) to the top.

Evelyn cuts off a final packet and places it face down onto the table.

"Evelyn, it's truly wonderful the way you've cut off such perfect small packets. I don't think I've ever seen anyone do that quite so well before. It's almost as though you're a professional. Let's see how you did."

Turn over the top card of each packet. Evelyn has succeeded in cutting the four aces!

"I don't know about the rest of you, but I don't think I'll *ever* play cards with Evelyn."

Note: The easy sleight described above is completely hidden. If, however, you feel sheepish about it, you can perform it while strolling about, chatting. In effect, you perform the move before anyone has reason to believe you're even going to perform a trick.

A Good Cut Of Chuck

I don't know who originated this trick, but it was shown to me by Chuck Golay, who I'm sure added touches of his own. It's that rare trick which requires little skill but gives the impression of incredible dexterity.

Fan through the deck, saying, "I'll need the four aces." When you come to a 5, cut the cards so that it becomes second from the top of the deck. "They have to be here somewhere." Toss the aces face up onto the table as you come to them.

Arrange the aces in a face-up row. Turn the deck face down. Cut from the top about a quarter of the cards and place the face-down packet below the ace on the left. (The packet is placed nearer to you.) Cut from the top about a third of the remaining cards and place the packet below the second ace from the right. Cut off about half of the remaining cards and place this packet below the second ace from the left. Place the remaining cards below the ace on the right. In other words, about a quarter of the deck is below each ace, with the original top portion of the deck being the pile on the left.

Pick up the packet on the left. (As you recall, the second card from the top of this packet is a 5.) Turn the packet face up and fan through the cards so that you can see which card is sixth from the original top. Pick up the ace on the left and place it to the right of this card. So the first ace is now seventh from the original top of the packet you're holding in your left hand (Illus. 54). Close up the packet.

Illus. 54

With your right hand, pick up the packet which is now on the left. Turn it face up and place it on top of the cards in your left hand. Pick up the ace on the left and place it on top of the cards in your left hand.

Fan back through the cards, showing how widely the two aces are separated. When you fan back to the face of the packet, get a break with the tip of your left little finger under the fourth card from the face. (See Below a Small Number from the Top, page 70.) Give the cards a double-cut, cutting the three cards above the break to the back of the face-up group. (See Double-Cut, page 18.)

Pick up the present packet on the left, turn it face up, and put it on top of the face-up cards in your left hand. Reach with your right hand to pick up the ace now on the left. As you do so, secure a break under the top card with your left little finger. (See Below the Top Card, page 70.) The action of reaching for the ace provides plenty of misdirection. Pick up the ace and place it face up on top of the packet. You're now holding a little-finger break beneath the top two cards of the packet. In a double-cut, move these two cards to the back of the face-up packet.

Handle the last packet and ace in exactly the same way as you did the third packet and ace.

The cards from the top are now in this order, x standing for any card:

$$x\,A\,x\,A\,x\,x\,x\,A\,x\,5\,x\,x\,x\,x\,A$$

Even up the cards and hold them up so that all can see that no cards are sticking out and that you're holding no breaks. *But don't say anything to that effect!*

Illus. 55

Turn the deck face down.

"Let's see if I can find any of the aces."

Lift the deck with your right hand. Turn your hand over, showing that the bottom card of the deck is not an ace. Place the deck face down into your left hand. Push off the top card with your left thumb. Take this card with your palm-down right hand, thumb at the inner end, fingers at the outer end. Lift it and show its face (Illus. 55). As you return the card to the top of the deck, you easily hold a break with your right thumb between the card and the rest of the deck. Your right fingers are holding the outer end of the deck, while the right thumb holds the break along with the inner end of the deck.

You're now going to perform a triple-cut, which is a variation of The Double-Cut, page 18. The left hand takes about a third of the cards from the bottom and places them on top, still retaining the break held by your right thumb. Again with the left hand, move a third of the cards from the bottom to the top. Now the left hand takes the remainder of the cards below the break and puts them on top. The upshot is that the top card which you showed is now on the bottom, and an ace is on top of the deck.

Turn the ace over, showing it, and place it face up onto the table.

To get a second ace, repeat all these moves. Finally, show the ace on top and place it onto the table next to the first ace.

Turn the deck face up and fan out several cards at the bottom, showing that there's no ace there. Turn the deck face down. Fan out three cards from the top. Take them in your right hand. Hold your hand up, displaying the faces (Illus. 56). As you replace them face

Illus. 56

down on top, get a break beneath them with the tip of your left little finger.

Once more you perform the triple-cut, bringing these three cards to the bottom. On top is an ace, which you turn over and deal onto the table next to the other two.

Lastly, you repeat the moves you used for the first two aces. This time, when you turn over the top card, it turns out to be a 5. "A five!" you declare, clearly disappointed. "We might as well use it."

Set the 5 aside face up. Slowly deal five cards from the top into a pile on the table, counting aloud. Turn over the last card dealt. It's the final ace.

"Thank goodness," you declare, placing the final ace next to the other three.

Two Hearts Beat as One

Wally Wilson developed a wonderful patter theme for this Stewart James origination. Incidentally, the printed descriptions of the original trick are not especially clear. My description includes Wally's patter theme and a few subtleties that I've added. I hope it's more coherent.

A small setup is required. On top of the deck you have the following values of any suits, except for the QH, which is the top card:

QH A 2 3 4 5 6 7 8 9 10

Start by picking two helpers, one male and one female. You might choose a married couple, or an engaged pair. It might be even more fun to pick two total strangers.

If you can, give the deck a shuffle, retaining the top stack, or perform a false cut. (See "False Cuts: sleight tips," pages 78 to 94.)

"Ladies and gentlemen, I'd like to conduct a compatibility test. I'll need a man and a woman. How about you, Mary . . . and you, Frank."

The two reluctantly join you. "Let's start with a brief quiz. Mary and Frank, what card do you believe would most symbolize love?"

They may come up with some amusing answers, or they may just stand there, stunned. If one of them says the QH, you're all set. Otherwise, you must elicit that answer. "It should definitely be a heart, don't you think?" If the correct answer comes early on, wonderful. Say, "Good choice. I believe that the queen of hearts is generally considered the card of love."

But if they fail to name the QH and keep naming hearts at random, you can make a joke of it as you provide obvious hints, like, "Perhaps it should be a female card." Subtle stuff like that. Eventually, you arrive at the QH.

"So you both agree that the queen of hearts is the card of love? What a great start! Now let's try an additional test."

Hand the deck to Mary, saying, "I'd like you to think of a number from one to ten. What's your number?" She tells you. "Good. Now please deal that number into a pile." As she does so, count aloud.

When she finishes, ask her to hand the rest of the deck to Frank. "I'd like you to think of a number, too, Frank—a different number from one to ten. What's your number?" Have him deal that number into a pile. You count aloud as he deals.

Take the deck from Frank and hang on to it.

You must make sure that the last pile dealt—in this instance, the pile dealt by Frank—goes on top of the other pile. Then the combined pile goes on top of the remainder of the deck. (Illus. 57 may help clarify this.) Obviously, you could pick up Frank's pile, place it on top of Mary's, and place the combined pile on top of the deck. But I devised a method which makes it appear that the participants actually choose the way the piles will be combined.

With your free hand, gesture toward the two piles on

MARY'S PILE

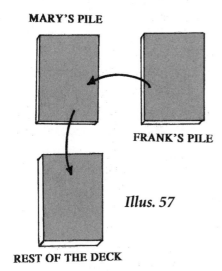

FRANK'S PILE

Illus. 57

REST OF THE DECK

the table as you say, "Mary, which pile do you want on top?" Let's say that she selects Frank's pile, which is the last pile dealt. You're delighted. Gesture that she is to place Frank's pile on top of her own. Then you pick up the combined pile and put it on top of the deck.

Suppose she chooses her own pile, the first one dealt. Without comment, pick up her pile and place it on top of the cards you're holding. Jokingly, continue, "Now which pile do you want on top?" Pause briefly with a smile; then pick up the other pile and place it on top of the deck.

The upshot, in either instance, is that the last pile dealt is on top of the deck, and the first pile is beneath it.

Let's suppose that Mary chose the number 4 and Frank the number 9. Turn to Frank. "Now you get a choice, Frank. Mary picked out the number four, and you picked the number nine. Which number should I deal out first?"

If Frank chooses the lower number, you'll do all the succeeding counting into a pile, one card on top of the other. If he chooses the higher number, you'll do all the deals by counting the cards into the right hand, taking one card under the other.

Let's say that Frank picks 4. Deal four cards into a pile on the table, counting them aloud. Turn over the last card dealt. It's a 9. "Look at that, Frank. We counted out Mary's number, which is four, and we ended up with a card that's the same as your number-nine."

Turn the 9 face down and replace the four cards on top of the deck. "So let's count out your number, Frank." Deal nine cards into a pile on the table, counting them aloud. Turn over the last card dealt. It's a 4. "Look at that, Mary. We counted out Frank's number, which is nine, and we ended up with a card that's the same as your number—four."

Turn the 4 face down and return the nine cards to the top of the deck.

"Maybe you guys are kind of compatible. Now, everyone, I have a tough math problem for you. What do we get when we add the two chosen numbers together?" Doubtless someone in the group will be able to total 9 and 4. And, if you're lucky, the total will be 13.

Deal 13 cards into a pile. Lift off the last card dealt, saying, "I wonder what this is." It's the QH. "The queen of hearts!" you declare. "The card of love. I hate to break it to you, but you two are really compatible."

Let's go back a bit. Remember when Frank chose either four or nine for you to count out? Well, fortunately, he chose the lower number, and everything worked out as described. But, as I mentioned, if he had chosen the higher number, the procedure would be different.

So let's say that Frank chose 9. You very deliberately count off the cards, but you take them one by one into your right hand, and you take them one under the other. This is so that they retain their order. In this instance, you count aloud as you take eight cards into your right hand, one under the other. You set this pile onto the table and turn over the ninth card, saying, "And here's the ninth card." It's a 4. Proceed with the recommended patter given above.

Turn the 4 face down on the deck. Pick up the eight-card pile and put it on top of the deck.

To be consistent, you take the cards one under the other to the end of the trick.

In this instance, you take three cards into your right hand, one under the other, counting aloud. Set this pile onto the table. Turn over the next card, announcing that it's the fourth one. It's a 9; comment on this. Return the 9 to the top of the deck. Put the three-card pile on top of the deck.

Your inquiry reveals that 9 plus 4 equals 13. You take 12 cards one under the other into your right hand, counting aloud. Set this pile onto the table. Turn over the next card, and conclude the trick as above.

False Shuffles: sleight tips

The Up-And-Down Shuffle

Hold the cards in the left hand in the dealing position. Push off the top card and take it into your right hand. Move your right hand forward (away from you) a few inches and push off the next card, taking it *below* the first one. You're now holding two cards. The top one extends about half its length beyond the lower card.

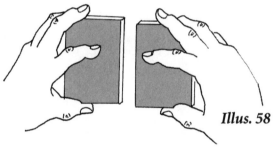

Illus. 58

Move the right hand back to its original position and take the third card below the other two; it should be more or less in line with the first card. Move the right hand forward again, taking the fourth card below the others; it should be more or less in line with the second card (Illus. 58). Continue through the packet. When you're finished, hold the upper group with your left

Illus. 59

hand as, with your right hand, you strip out the lower group from the others (Illus. 59). This group goes on top of the cards remaining in your left hand.

Notes

(1) Depending on the trick, in the first move of the shuffle you may move the top card down or toward you, the next card up, the next card down, and so forth.

(2) Depending on the trick, when you strip out the lower group (the cards nearest you), these will sometimes go below the cards you hold in your left hand.

The Charlier Shuffle

This unusual shuffle—invented, I presume, by a guy named Charlier—gives the deck a complete cut. Since a complete cut retains the basic order of a deck of cards, this shuffle is perfect for tricks using a completely setup

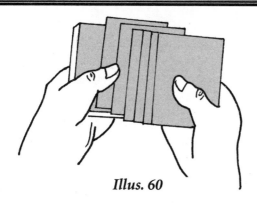

Illus. 60

deck. It is extraordinarily sloppy looking, which adds to its effectiveness.

With the left thumb, push off a half dozen cards or so from the top, taking them in the right hand (Illus. 60). From the bottom of the cards in the left hand, push off several with the left fingers (Illus. 61). This group is placed on top of the cards in the right hand (Illus. 62).

Illus. 61

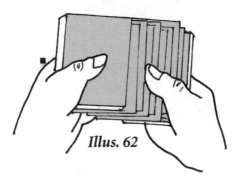

Illus. 62

Again, push off several from the top with the left thumb and take these on the bottom of the cards in the right hand. Next, a small pile from the bottom of the left-hand bunch goes on top of the cards in the right hand. Continue alternating like this until all the cards have been transferred to the right hand. Even up the cards. The deck has been given a cut, but the cards are still in their basic order.

I often use my variation of this procedure to retain all the cards in their exact order from top to bottom.

As described above, start by pushing off a half dozen cards from the top and taking them in the right hand. Next, cards are pushed off from the bottom with the left fingers. This packet is placed on top of those in the right hand, about an inch to an inch-and-a-half forward of those already there.

As you continue the shuffle, packets that are placed on top are gradually placed farther back until they are even with the cards taken underneath. At the conclusion, the bottom card of the packet jutting from the front of the deck is the original bottom card. In fact, this bottom card may well be jutting out all by itself. In any instance, place all the cards into the left hand, without straightening them out.

After the "shuffle," you must cut at this "jutting-out" point, bringing the bottom card back to its original position. This, of course, restores the entire deck to its original order.

So, as the last move of the shuffle, with your right hand pick up all the cards above, including the original bottom card. Place this group below the lower cards.

Even up the deck.

Note: Before you start shuffling, it's well to make an appropriate remark, like, "I hope you don't mind, but I'm going to mess these cards up a bit," or, "I need to practice a new shuffle I just learned; it's called 'a complete mess.'"

The One-Two-Three Shuffle

I developed this pseudo-shuffle some time ago. It's quite useful for retaining the exact order of a small group of cards while apparently mixing them. It also can be used to move a particular card to a specific position in a packet without resorting to serious sleight of hand. I recommend its use in two of the tricks in this book, and it could be used in others as well.

Let's suppose you have a packet of 12 cards and you wish to retain its exact order. You must transfer 12 cards to the bottom of the packet, moving one, two, or three cards at a time.

You may do it any way you wish, as long as you move 12 cards. Here's one possibility:

Fan off two cards and put them on the bottom, saying mentally, "Two."

Fan off three cards and put them on the bottom, saying mentally, "Five." (You added three to the two.)

Fan off one card and put it on the bottom, saying mentally, "Six."

Fan off one card and put it on the bottom, saying mentally, "Seven."

Fan off three cards and put them on the bottom, saying mentally, "Ten."

Fan off two cards and put them on the bottom, saying mentally, "Twelve."

All done, and the cards are back in their original order.

Suppose you know the bottom card of that 12-card

packet and that you'd like to move it to the third position from the top. Subtract 3 from 12, getting 9. You must transfer nine cards from the top to the bottom, moving one, two, or three cards at a time.

Suppose you know the top card of that 12-card packet and that you'd like to move it to the fifth position from the top. Obviously, you want to put four cards on top of that known card, so you subtract 4 from 12, getting 8. Transfer eight cards to the bottom, using the usual method.

The key to success with this shuffle is to appear casual; the spectators should have no hint that you're counting to yourself.

False Shuffles: tricks

Am I Blue?

A bit of preparation is necessary. For purposes of patter, you must use a red-backed deck. Note the bottom card of the deck. From a blue-backed deck, take a duplicate of that card and place it on the bottom of the red-backed deck.

The situation as you begin: You have, say, a king of hearts second from the bottom of your red-backed deck. On the bottom, you have another king of hearts, which has a blue back.

Fan through the cards, asking Lois to choose one. (Make sure you do not get to the bottom and reveal the blue-backed card.) As she shows the card around, close up the fan. Perform the Hindu Shuffle, as follows. Start with the deck in the dealing position in your left hand. With your palm-down right hand, grasp the cards at the near narrow end. Bring the deck toward you with your right hand, allowing your left fingers to draw off a small packet from the top (Illus. 63). This packet falls into your left hand. Draw off another packet, letting it fall onto the one in your left hand. Continue until only a

Illus. 63.

small packet remains in your right hand. Drop this on top of the others.

At about the middle of the deck, stop and ask Lois to replace her card. Hold out the cards in your left hand for the return. Drop the card in your right hand on top. The blue-backed card is now above the chosen card.

"I wonder if you'd mind blowing on the deck." After she does so, say, "Blow a little harder, please." If this is evoking amusement, you might ask her to blow even harder. "Oh, my! I think you blew too hard." Fan through the deck to the blue-backed card. Cut at the point to bring the blue-backed card to the top. "You *really* blew. In fact, you turned one of the cards blue." Ask, "What was the card you chose?"

Lois tells you. Do the double-lift, demonstrating that the blue-backed card is, in fact, the one she selected. Turn the double card face down and deal the top card (blue-backed) onto the table.

At this point, you have a blue-backed king of hearts

face down on the table and the duplicate of that card on the bottom of the deck.

"Let's try it again," you say. You'll now perform the Hindu Shuffle force as follows. You have your force card on the bottom of the deck. With your first move, you not only withdraw a packet from the top, but you also cling to a small packet on the bottom with your left thumb and left fingers. The packet from the top falls on top of this packet. Complete the shuffle in the usual way. Apparently you've performed a regular Hindu shuffle; actually, the bottom several cards remain exactly as they were. This means, of course, that the force card is still on the bottom. Perform this maneuver a few times.

"Tell me when to stop," you direct Lois. Then commence the Hindu Shuffle. When she says stop, show her the bottom card of those in your right hand. Replace these cards on top.

Repeat the business of having her blow on the deck. "Let's see if it worked." Fan through the deck, but this time there's no blue-backed card. Close up the cards and have her blow on the deck again, but once more you fail to find a blue-backed card.

Look puzzled. "I think I know what happened. What's the name of your card?" She names it. "Just as I thought. The king of hearts is a troublemaker, and a really mixed-up card. It can't make up its mind whether it wants to be blue or red." Turn over the card on the table. "See what I mean?"

Pause for a moment. Pick up the blue-backed king of hearts and place it in your pocket, saying, "We'd better get rid of that little rascal."

Further thoughts

Perhaps you're wondering, "As I proceed with other tricks, won't people notice that the king of hearts is back in the deck?" They might, and if they comment, you say, "Oh, yes, that little rascal is back." On one occasion, a spectator said to me, "But you put the five of spades in your pocket." My reply was, "Oh, that was a different five of spades," and I went into the next trick.

Yes, it occasionally works well to tell spectators the truth. Since you're a magician, they're unlikely to believe you anyway.

Note: This clever trick was shown to me by Wally Wilson.

Five-Card Turnabout

Five cards, ace through 5, are dealt out in order. But with a wave of the hand, you cause them to reverse their order. Milt Kort did not invent the trick, but he developed much of the handling and the basic logic behind it.

Remove from the deck these cards: AD, 2D, 3D, 4D, 5D. (Clearly, any suit will do.) As you toss the cards face up onto the table, say, "I have trouble understanding a weird shuffle I heard about. Maybe you can help me."

Pick up the ace and place it face up in your hand. On top of it, place the face-up 5. Follow this with the 2, the 4, and the 3. When you turn the packet face down, they will be in this order, from the top: A, 5, 2, 4, 3. It's easy to remember because the order is logical:

Rather than consider the ace as a high card, think of it as a one. The order then goes low to high, low to high, and then middle. First , you go lowest to highest (A to 5), then from second lowest to second highest (2 to 4), and finally to the middle (3).

Turn the packet face down. "Now I'll show you the weird shuffle I mentioned." Start fanning through the cards from top to the bottom. As you do this, you perform an abbreviated version of the up-and-down shuffle. (See The Up-and-Down Shuffle, pages 95 to 96.) The first card goes up, the second down, and so forth. You end up with two cards sticking out the bottom of the packet. These two are stripped out by the right hand

and placed on top of the packet. From the top down, the cards now run 5, 4, A, 2, 3.

Repeat this "shuffle" three times (four times in all); the cards are now in the same position as when you started. As you repeat this up-down shuffle, keep repeating, "I don't know if I'm mixing these up or sorting them out."

When you're finished, add, "This is the strangest shuffle."

Deal the top card face down onto the table. Place the next card under the packet. Deal the next card to the right of the first card on the table. The next card goes to the bottom of the packet. Continue until all five cards are in a row on the table. Turn them over, showing that they run in order from your left to right.

Gather up the cards one by one, placing them face up in your left hand. This time, you pick up the cards in their natural order, starting with the ace, following with the 2, and so on. *Except* that you pick up the 5 third and the 3 last. In other words, as you pick up the cards, you exchange the positions of the 5 and 3. So, when you turn the pile face down, the cards will run from the top A, 2, 5, 4, 3.

As you gather up the cards, say, "I would love that shuffle if only it were consistent. But when I do it, I have no idea of what's going to happen." By this time the cards should have been gathered and turned face down.

You again perform your weird "shuffle." Now, however, you do it only three times. And don't forget to say, each time, "I don't know if I'm mixing these up or sorting them out." After three "shuffles," this will be the order of the cards: 5, A, 2, 4, 3.

At the end of this third up-and-down shuffle, you're holding two cards at the sides in your right hand. When you place the two cards on top, get a small break below them with the tip of your left little finger. This is by way of preparation for a double-lift. You will find the basic move under When Putting Cards on Top of the Deck, page 71. You should probably check it out before proceeding with this variation.

As described, you obtain a break beneath the top two cards with your left little finger. Your left thumb is resting on the left side of the deck. With the palm-down right hand, you grip the packet on the ends, near the right side. The first finger is on top, the second finger grips the cards at the outer end; the thumb, at the inner end, takes over the break held by your left little finger (Illus. 64).

Slide your right hand to the left side of the packet; the right thumb retains and expands the break below the

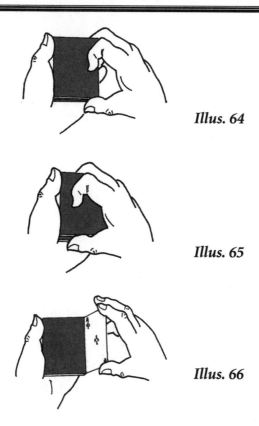

Illus. 64

Illus. 65

Illus. 66

top two cards (Illus. 65). Display the ace by swinging the top two cards in an arc to the right, as though opening the back cover of a book (Illus. 66). Say, "Ace," as you return the double-card to its original face-down position. Deal the top card (the 5) face down onto the table. Just as you did before, move the new top card to the bottom of the packet.

Spread the four cards to show that everything is fair and aboveboard. Actually, you are just making it easier to once more get a break beneath the top two cards with your left little finger. Close up the cards. Once more, perform the double-lift as described above. This time, you display the 2. Return the double-card to its original face-down position, saying, "Two." Deal the top card (the 4) face down onto the table, to your right of the first card. Move the new top card to the bottom of the packet.

To be consistent, spread the three remaining cards, showing them. Close them up. Display the 3 in precisely the same manner as you did the first two cards. Turn it face down onto the packet, saying, "Three." Deal it onto the table to the right of the other two cards.

You are now holding two cards. Move the top one below the other one. Make a show of spreading the two cards. Put the top one on the table to the right of the other cards, saying, "Four." Place the last one down to the right of all, saying, "Five."

You now use some "time misdirection." Address one of the group, "Do you think you could do that weird shuffle?" Whatever the answer, say, "Maybe you could; I don't know. Sometimes there's something magical about it. Take a look at what happens." Point to the table. "I put these down in order: ace, two, three, four, five. Now look at them."

Starting at your left, turn the cards over, showing them to be in reverse order: 5, 4, 3, 2, ace.

Note: Instead of performing the double-lift as described above, you may substitute any double-lift you're familiar with.

Five Choice Cards

Alex Elmsley, one of the all-time great innovators in card magic, came up with this unique approach to a standard trick. I have made some slight changes.

Fan through the face-up deck, saying, "Let's see, we'll need five red and five black cards."

Therefore, you remove ten cards from the deck—five red, five black. You remove them one at a time, placing them into a face-up pile on the table in a particular order. The order is easy to remember. You start with a pair of alternating colors. Let's say you place a red card down face up. On top of it, you must place a black card. So face up on the table, you have: R-B.

The next four pairs will each contain a red and a black, but each will begin with the same color as the last card placed down. In this instance, the last card placed down was a black. Therefore, the next card you place down must also be a black. And it is followed by a red: R-B B-R.

The next pair? You've already guessed. It begins with a red. Thus: R-B B-R R-B.

All five pairs will be as follows: R-B B-R R-B B-R R-B.

So you will either have the above order: R B B R R B B R R B. Or you will have this order: B R R B B R R B B R.

Either order will do just fine.

Pick up the pile of cards and turn it face down.

Raymond has agreed to assist you, so you must explain, "Raymond, you'll choose five of these cards." Take off the top card. "If you choose this card, it goes onto the table." Deal it onto the table, but keep your grip on it.

Replace it on top of the packet, still retaining your grip.

"If you don't choose the top card, it goes on the bottom." Move the card to the bottom, and then back to the top.

"Let's mix the cards up a bit so that neither of us knows which is where." You're about to give the packet an up-and-down shuffle. (See The Up-and-Down Shuffle, pages 95 to 96.) But first, ask Raymond, "Should the first card go up or go down?" Do as he indicates; then complete the up-and-down portion of the shuffle. Strip out the lower packet. "Should this packet go on top of the other packet or below it?" Do as he indicates.

Place the packet onto the table. "You'd better give them a cut, Raymond." The cards are given as many complete cuts as desired.

Pick up the packet, saying, "I'd better mix them some more." Give the packet another up-and-down shuffle, giving Raymond the same choices as before.

It seems impossible but the top five cards are all of the same color, and, of course, so are the bottom five cards.

Put the cards behind your back. Bring the top one forward, holding it face down. "Raymond, do you want this one, or not?" If he wants it, place it onto the table (or on his hand). In the latter instance, say, "Don't peek."

If the card is rejected, place it back on top. Fiddle around a bit and bring out the same card. (Presumably, you've placed it on the bottom.)

Continue like this until Raymond has chosen five cards.

"Every once in a blue moon, Raymond, a spectator proves that he has exceptional ESP by choosing cards that are all the same color. Let's see what you have?"

He turns his cards over. Sure enough, he has chosen all of the same color. You bring the other cards forward. And, of course, you have all of the other color.

Notes

(1) You might do the trick this way. Sneak a peek at the bottom card of the packet after you perform the last up-and-down shuffle. The bottom five cards will all be of the same color. Ask Raymond, "Which do you prefer, Raymond—red or black?" Suppose he says red. If the bottom card was red, you let him choose from the bottom five cards. If it was black, you let him choose from the top five cards.

At the end, express surprise at his ability to choose the exact color that he wanted.

(2) How do you end up with the blacks and reds separated? Simple, really. After the first up-and-down shuffle, the colors alternate. The complete cuts do not affect this order. And the next up-and-down shuffle separates the blacks and reds.

(3) The cards cannot be cut before you make your first up-and-down shuffle. This will destroy the proper order.

My Time Is Your Time

Wally Wilson showed me yet another clock trick. This one is extraordinarily deceptive.

Start by handing Jack the deck and asking him to give it a shuffle. When he's done, say, "It's no secret, Jack, that the number 12 is quite significant. For instance, there are the 12 signs of the Zodiac, the 12 months in a year, the 12 hours shown on the clock, and so on. So, please count off 12 cards into a pile."

After he does so, take the rest of the deck from him. "Please pick up your 12 cards, Jack."

You have placed the remainder of the deck into your left hand, preparatory to making an overhand shuffle. As Jack picks up his cards, you let the deck tilt slightly back toward the palm of your left hand (Illus. 67). Casually look down at your hands, sneaking a peek at the bottom card of the deck.

This is important: Begin to give the cards an overhand shuffle *before* you say, "Shuffle your cards like this."

Jack shuffles his packet. You complete your overhand shuffle by shuffling off the last several cards individually, thus bringing the card you peeked at to the top of the deck.

(You must know the name of the top card of those

you're holding. Clearly, any other sneaky way you want to do it is just fine.)

Set your cards onto the table. Avert your head and tell Jack, "Please cut off some of your cards and put them into your pocket. But don't pay attention to the number as you do this."

When he's done, say, "Put the rest of your cards on top of the deck and even up the deck."

You once more face the group.

"Neither of us knows how many cards you have in your pocket, right? Now I'd like you to pick up the deck and count out 12 cards, dealing them into a pile."

He does this.

"Set the rest of the deck aside. Pick up the pile of 12 cards and deal it out, forming a clock. The first card will be at one o'clock, and the last will be at 12 o'clock."

The clock has been formed. Move the card marking 12 o'clock an inch or two out of line as you comment, "So this is 12 o'clock."

Turn away. "I'd like you to take those cards from your pocket, Jack, and count them. But don't tell me the number."

He counts the cards.

"You have your number? Look at the card that lies at that time. For example, if you had four cards in your pocket, you'd look at the card that lies at four o'clock. Show the card around and then replace it face down. When you're done, put the cards that you had in your pocket back on top of the deck."

You turn back and reveal the chosen card any way you wish.

Remember that card you peeked at? Well, that's the one he chose. You can have him gather up all the cards and shuffle them. Then you can go through the deck and locate the card, or else read the spectator's mind.

My favorite conclusion is this: Before I turn back, I have the spectator gather up all the cards and shuffle them. When I face the group, I take the deck, riffle the ends a few times, and then rub it against my wristwatch.

"Since you used a clock in choosing a card, maybe my timepiece will help me identify it." I set the deck onto the table.

I hold my wristwatch to my ear and listen to it as it

slowly gives me the color, the suit, and the value of the selected card.

For Openers

Although you may do the tricks in any order (except for the last one), I highly recommend that you present this one first.

Start by having a number of spectators give the deck a complete cut. Then ask Greg to give you a hand.

"Greg, I'd like you to cut off about a third of the cards and place them right here." Point to a spot to your left of the deck. Note the arrow in Illus. 68.

"Now please cut off about half of the remaining cards and place them right here." Point to a spot to your right of the two piles. Note the arrow in Illus. 69.

"Get ready for real magic. I'm going to name each of these cards." Turn over one of the cards, leaving it on top of its packet. Name the card.

Do the same with the other two piles.

"Is that magic, or what? Definitely 'or what,' right? Anyone can name a card by turning it over and looking at it. Let me see if I can concentrate and name some face-down cards, like the ones at the bottom of each of these piles."

For clarity, let's mentally number the piles 1, 2, and 3, going from your left to right.

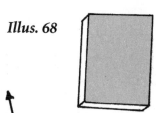

Illus. 68

Note the face-up card on top of Pile 3. The one that precedes it in the setup order is the bottom card of Pile 1.

Let's say that the top card of Pile 3 is the 3H. In the sequence, a K always precedes a 3. And in the CHSD sequence, clubs comes just before hearts. Therefore, the card at the bottom of Pile 1 is the KC. After pondering for several seconds, touch Pile 1 and name its bottom card. Turn the pile over, showing that you're correct. After everyone has seen the bottom card of Pile 1, turn the pile over again.

Note the face-up card of Pile 1. The card that

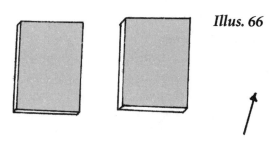

Illus. 66

precedes it in order is the card on the bottom of Pile 2. Reveal this card precisely as you did the first one.

And the card at the bottom of Pile 3 precedes the face-up card on Pile 2. You reveal this card as you did the others.

While some spectators are gasping and others are muttering about fitting you for a dunking stool, turn the face-up cards over on their respective piles. Then place Pile 3 onto Pile 2. Once you've done this, it doesn't matter whether Pile 1 goes on top or not. The basic order of the setup is restored.

Incidentally, it improves the trick and tends to avoid suspicion if you actually miss. For example, suppose you know that the card on the bottom of Pile 2 is the nine of clubs. You might say, "I know it's a dark card, but I'm not sure which suit it is. I'll say spades." Think a bit more. "Yes, six of spades." Show the card. "I was afraid I might miss the suit. And wouldn't you know, I got the value upside down."

My suggestion is that you get one card absolutely right, preferably the third card. One you should miss as described above, and one you should get the value right but miss on the suit. Who knows, maybe you do have some sort of mental powers. After all, you almost got all three right.

Best of all, however, is that the notion of a stacked deck is stifled.

To further allay any possible suspicion, before the next trick give the deck a Charlier Shuffle, described on page 96.

Note: If in the heat of action you should forget which card denotes the card at the bottom of which pile, simply review the cutting process in your mind. If you have to do this, you'll simply appear to be straining your brain as you try to squeeze the ESP out of it.

It's a Setup!

Stewart James invented an intriguing prediction trick using dominoes. I have adapted the trick to playing cards and have tossed in a few ideas of my own.

In advance, stack nine cards on top of the deck. From the top down, these are the values; the suits are irrelevant:

8 A 6 3 5 7 4 9 2

If you can, give the deck a false shuffle or a false cut, retaining the position of at least the top nine cards.

Say, "I'll need to find a prediction card."

Fan through the deck with the faces of the cards toward yourself, apparently looking for a prediction card. Actually, you're counting the cards. Note the 15th card from the bottom. Go through the rest of the deck to find the card which matches this in color and value. Remove this card from the deck and set it aside face down, announcing that it's your prediction card. Make sure you don't take this card from the bottom 15 cards, or from the top nine. If you can't find the exact mate, simply take out a card of the same value. (Occasionally, all the other possibilities will be among the bottom 15 or the top nine. When this occurs, chances are a matching card will be among the bottom 15. Take a card from the rest of the deck, study it, shake your head no, and replace the card among the bottom 15. Study the cards further. Finally remove the appropriate matching card from the bottom 15 and place it onto the table.)

Set the deck down, saying, "I've made my prediction; I'll not touch the deck again."

Ask Rose to help out. "Please pick up the deck, Rose. Now you're going to get a choice. You can either deal cards face down from the top of the deck, or you can turn the deck over and deal them face up from the bottom. Which will it be—top or bottom?"

Let's suppose she chooses to deal from the bottom. Say, "Please turn the deck over, Rose, and deal the cards into a pile."

Make sure she has dealt several cards past 15 before you say, "Stop whenever you wish."

When she stops, ask her to turn the pile face down.

"Rose, we're going to choose a number down in that pile in the fairest possible way. Turn the cards you're holding face down. Deal the top three cards into a face-down row, going from left to right. Below them, deal the next three out in the same way. Below that last three, deal three more in the same way."

The face-down cards will be as shown in Illus. 70. Notice that the values are shown for clarity, but the cards are actually face down, and they form a so-called "magic square": Each row, each column, and each diagonal adds to 15.

"Please set the rest of the cards you're holding over here." Indicate a position some distance from the pile she dealt out from the bottom. "Now I'd like you to choose any row or any column." As you say this, with your finger indicate first the rows and then the columns. "In fact, you can choose either of the diagonals." With your finger, indicate the two diagonals.

Pass your finger over the rows, columns, and diagonals as you say, "You have one, two, three, four, five, six, seven, eight possible choices. Which do you select?"

When she indicates her choice, have her turn over the

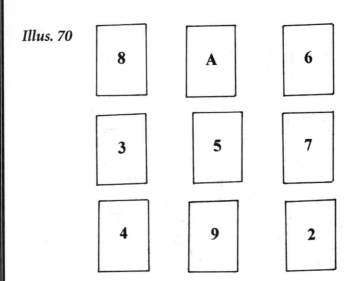

appropriate three cards. "Add those up, please, Rose. What do you get?"

She tells you 15.

"Please pick up the other pile and deal off 15 cards into a pile."

After she deals off the 15 cards, tell Rose, "Please turn over the last card you dealt." She does. "Now pick it up and show it around, please." As she does this, gather up all the other cards on the table except for the prediction card. Casually give these cards a little shuffle as you say,

"Would you please turn over my prediction card to see if there's a match." She does, and there is.

But let's go back. What if Rose decides to deal from the top? Surely you've figured it out already. If she deals from the top, she deals the top three cards into a row, the next three into a row beneath them, and the last three into another row.

As before, you tell her, "Please turn the deck over, Rose, and deal the cards into a pile."

She should deal several cards past 15 before you say, "Stop whenever you wish."

When she stops, ask her to turn the pile face down.

Then it's back to the nine cards. And the conclusion follows, as described above.

Only the Beginning

This started out with my attempting to improve an old Stewart James trick. It ended up with my modifying the original considerably and creating an additional version. This, I think, resulted in twice the mystery. But what do I know?

Say that you'll remove all the clubs from the deck and do so. Patter about the two red jacks being members of the Royal Canadian Mounted Police, and that everyone knows that they always get their man. Toss the two red jacks face up onto the table.

You are going to use only the 13 clubs and the two red jacks, so set the rest of the deck aside.

Diane's father is a magician, so she should be an excellent helper.

Hand her the clubs. "Please fan through them face up, Diane, and pick one out. It doesn't matter if we all see what it is." She picks out a card—let's say the 6C. "Turn the cards face down and put the six of clubs face down on top. So your selection, the six of clubs, is the criminal. And he'll try to hide from the Mounties."

Take the packet from Diane and perform an up-and-down shuffle—the first card going up, the second down, and so on. (See "The Up-and-Down Shuffle," pages 95 to 96.) When you're done, strip out the lowermost cards and place them on top of the others. Pick up one of the face-up jacks from the table, turn it face down, and place it on top. "So one of the Mounties starts his search."

Illus. 71

126

Repeat the up-and-down shuffle.

Pick up the other face-up jack, turn it face down, and place it on top. "And now another Mountie takes up the search. Can the six of clubs possibly escape?"

Repeat the up-and-down shuffle. Set the packet face down onto the table. "Let's really make things tough for the Mounties." Have Diane give the packet a complete cut. You may let others cut the packet, as well.

"We should really mix them a little more." Give the packet one more up-and-down shuffle.

"So let's see how the forces of justice did." Fan through the cards face up so that all can see the faces. Sure enough, the chosen card is surrounded by the two jacks. Be scrupulously careful as you pull the block of three from the deck and set it on the table for inspection (Illus. 71).

Brief review:

(1) Spectator places a card on top of the clubs.

(2) Up-and-down shuffle, lower cards going on top.

(3) Jack goes on top of the packet.

(4) Up-and-down shuffle.

(5) Jack goes on top of the packet.

(6) Up-and-down shuffle.

(7) Spectators cut the packet.

(8) A fourth up-and-down shuffle.

COIN TRICKS

Vanishes: sleight tips

The magician shows a coin, and it disappears. This is unquestionably the basic coin trick. You should have several ways to accomplish this.

French Drop

One of the oldest of all coin sleights is the French Drop. Many people are familiar with it. Done properly, it's an effective, deceptive vanish.

For most of these tricks, the type of coin or coins you use is irrelevant. I recommend, however, that you use a fairly large coin, either a quarter or a half-dollar, when you manipulate a single coin.

Let's try the basic sleight.

With the left hand turned palm up and fingers curled in, hold the coin between the first two fingers and the thumb.

The right hand is palm down as it approaches from above.

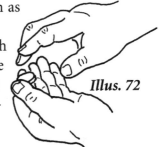

The right thumb is beneath the coin and the fingers above it, and you close your right hand into a fist as you, presumably, take the coin.

Illus. 72

Actually, you simply spread the first finger and thumb of the left hand slightly apart, dropping the coin onto the cupped fingers of the left hand. The right hand, which now supposedly holds the coin, continues to move forward.

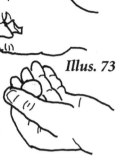

Illus. 73

This is one of the simplest coin sleights and probably the best known, but the vast majority of those who attempt it, do it badly. Perhaps you've seen someone perform the sleight and present both closed fists, asking you to pick out the one containing the coin.

Sleights should be performed smoothly and naturally. How do you learn to perform a sleight *naturally*? Practice by actually taking the coin in your right fist instead of performing the sleight. Next, perform the French Drop. Then, actually take the coin. Continue alternating until, when you perform the sleight, you precisely duplicate the action of taking the coin. I don't recommend practicing in front of a mirror (some performers tend to narrow their eyes so they won't see the sleight, and carry this habit over into performance), bud do check periodically to see if the sleight looks natural. Be sure to try *both* ways in front of the mirror.

You've performed the French Drop, and the right fist has moved forward, ostensibly with the coin. What about that left hand? There's a tendency to want to hide the coin, to close the left hand; resist that temptation. Simply drop the cupped left hand naturally to your side. *Don't close the hand*; there's no need to, since the coin is secure there. No one will see it; attention is on the right hand. *But* the coin had better be produced, and soon.

Here's another possibility. Immediately after you ostensibly take the coin with the right hand, point to the right hand with the left forefinger, and then let the hand drop to your side.

French Drop For One

This is a mystifying variation of the French Drop, but it's best performed for an audience of one. Ideally, the spectator will be seated and you'll be standing. Otherwise, you'd have to hold the coin rather high, because it must be held close to the spectator's eye level.

The coin (preferable a fifty-cent piece) is held between the thumb and first finger of the palm-up left hand, about a foot from the spectator.

The right hand approaches from above, and the tips of the right second and third fingers push against the right side of the coin, pivoting it around.

As you complete the revolution of the coin (heads is now where the tails was) several things happen. You loosen your grip on the coin with the left thumb and first finger, and the coin drops onto

Illus. 74

the cupped fingers of the left hand, and you press your right thumb against the right second and third fingers as though holding the coin.

Raise the right hand in the air, with the back of your hand to the spectator. Snap your fingers, showing that the coin has disappeared. With your left hand, produce the coin with one of the methods given in *Reappearances*, pages 165 to 186.

Easy Vanish

There are several ways of pretending to place a coin in one hand while actually retaining it in the other. The following method is one of the easiest to perform, yet it's completely deceptive.

Any size coin will do for this stunt. First, practice the actual placement of the coin, then do the sleight.

Hold both hands out face up, a coin resting on the pads of the second and third fingers of the right hand.

Move the right thumb so that it holds the coin in

Illus. 75

place, turn the hand palm down and raise the hand so that it's above and to the right of the left hand (Illus. 75).

Place the coin in the middle of the left palm.

Let go of the coin, and as you withdraw the right hand, fingers still together, close the fingers of the left hand on the coin. As your right hand withdraws, the closing fingers of the left hand should brush lightly against the back of the right fingers.

When your right hand is a few inches from your left hand, cup the second, third, and fourth fingers, leaving the first finger extended. Tap your left wrist once with your right forefinger, and let your right hand drop naturally to your side. Gradually open the left hand, and, sure enough, the coin is there.

Practice the actual placement several times before you attempt the sleight. Do it very deliberately. You could do a

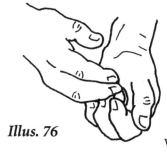

Illus. 76

leisurely two-count. Count "one" for placing the coin in the palm, and "two" for tapping the wrist with the forefinger.

For the sleight, you do everything in exactly the same way, except that at the step where you let go of the coin, simply hang on to it; keep it between the thumb and the second and third fingers of the right hand. Don't forget to tap your wrist with your forefinger; this creates the impression that your right hand is empty. Let your right hand drop to your side.

Now the closed left hand presumably holds the coin, but the coin is actually in the right hand. All that remains is the disclosure of the disappearance, followed instantly by a magical reappearance.

Combined Vanish

For certain tricks, the following vanish is the sleight of choice, for instance, for Leg Work, pages 163 to 164.

Again, both hands are displayed, palms up. A coin lies on the right fingers approximately one-half inch from the tips. Bring the right hand over, and in front of, the left hand, with the tips of the right fingers under and touching the back of the tips of the left fingers

Illus. 77

(Illus. 77).

As the right hand moves up and back, closing the left fingers and presumably dropping the coin, the right thumb grips the coin (Illus. 78).

The right hand continues back a few inches. Cup the second, third, and fourth fingers of the right hand and tap the left wrist with the extended forefinger. In some tricks, this last tapping move may be omitted.

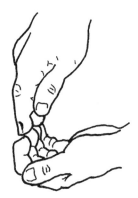

Illus. 78

A Common Vanish

Start by holding out the left hand palm up and displaying a coin on your right fingertips (Illus. 79). Notice that the coin does not overlap the fingertips; this is important.

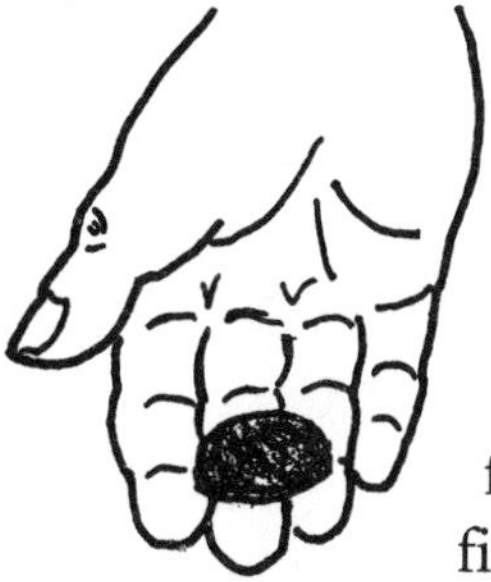

Illus. 79

Place your right thumb on top of the coin, securing it in the right hand (Illus. 80). Tilt the left hand back a bit as you turn the right hand palm down and bring it forward of the left hand and above it. The tips of the right fingers should be lightly touching the fingernails of the left hand (Illus. 81).

Bring your right hand toward you, more or less closing up the left hand by gently pushing the fingers back and, presumably, dropping the coin in the process. But, of course, you're not dropping the coin; you're still retaining your thumb grip.

Keep looking at your left hand as you drop the right hand to your side. When your right hand is about midway in its descent to your side, you can release the thumb grip because the coin will naturally fall onto your semi-cupped

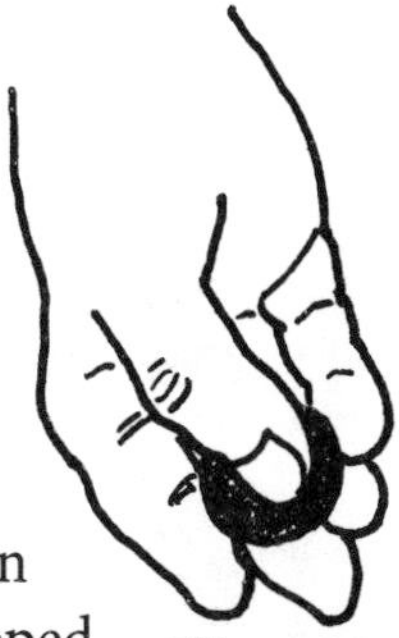

Illus. 80

fingers. By cupping your fingers a bit more, you'll find that you are gripping the coin in a finger palm.

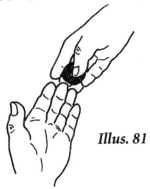

Illus. 81

Flip Vanish

This Milt Kort invention is a very clever change of pace from more conventional vanishes.

Tell the audience, "I'd like to show you something very mysterious. Centuries ago in China, a sorcerer discovered that if you handle a coin in this peculiar way, something strange will happen."

Place a coin onto the tips of the right fingers. Put your left hand onto the right palm (Illus. 82).

Move both hands upward in a quick movement, flipping the coin into the

Illus. 82

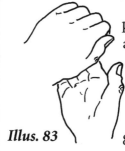

Illus. 83

palm of the left hand. The move is not at all difficult; it can probably be accomplished on your first attempt.

Revolve your left hand clockwise, starting to close it. As you do so, drop the coin onto the right fingers (Illus. 83). Close your left hand completely.

As soon as the coin hits the right fingers, turn the right hand counterclockwise and close the second, third, and fourth fingers over the coin. Extend the right forefinger, pointing it at the closed left hand (Illus. 84).

Show that the coin has vanished, and then make it reappear.

This move is not "angle-proof," meaning that unless you place yourself in a particular position in relation to the audience, someone might see the move. Therefore, after working on the move for a while, do it in front of a mirror to make sure you know what position you should take in relation to the audience.

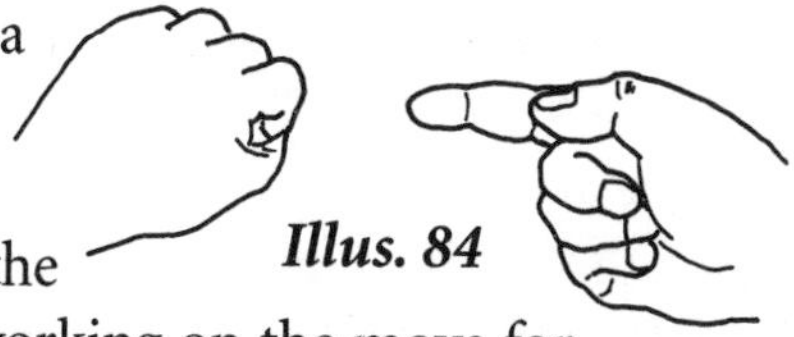

Illus. 84

Small Coin Vanish

Some time ago, I tried David Ginn's method for making a small coin vanish, but found it quite difficult. So I worked

Illus. 85

out a simplified method that works well for me.

I think the sleight becomes quite easy if we go through the individual steps:

(1) Hold the left hand out, palm up.

(2) Also hold the right hand out, palm up, with a small coin balanced on the first finger and the other fingers closed up (Illus. 85). Note that the thumb is pressed against the side of the second finger.

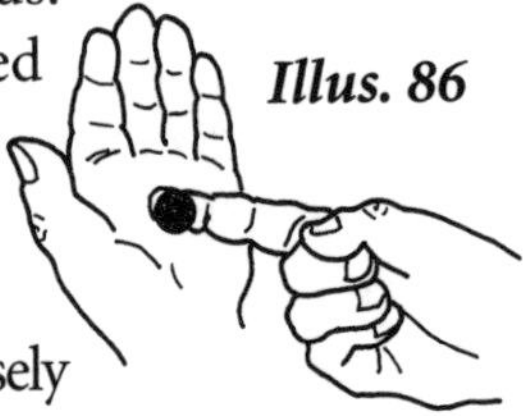

Illus. 86

(3) Place the right first finger on the palm of the left hand (Illus. 86).

(4) Turn the left hand clockwise, loosely cupping it as you do so (Illus. 87).

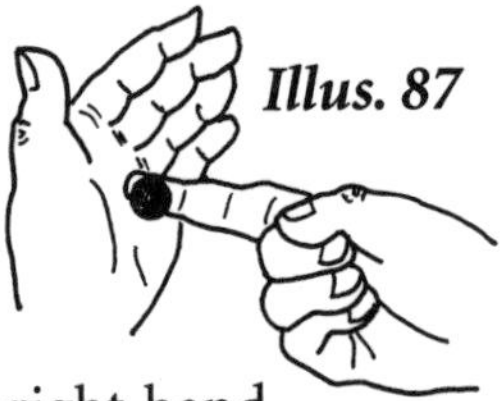

Illus. 87

(5) As soon as the left hand conceals the first finger of the right hand, revolve the right hand slightly in a counterclockwise direction. At the same time, bend the first finger of the right hand inward. This enables you to press on the coin with your right thumb (Illus. 88).

Illus. 88

(6) The right thumb proceeds to slide the coin to the right until it is concealed behind the right fingers. (The arrow in Illus. 89 indicates where the coin is hidden.) At the same time, the left hand closes completely and moves away to the

left, presumably taking the coin with it.

Illus. 89

(7) Follow your left hand with your eyes as you let the right hand drop to your side and the coin fall into your slightly cupped fingers.

Blow on the closed left hand and then open it to show that the coin has vanished.

Vanishes: tricks

Heads Up

Use a fifty-cent piece or a quarter for this stunt. A tricky movement is required, but you should master it after five or ten minutes of practice.

The idea is to convince spectators that you have a double-headed coin.

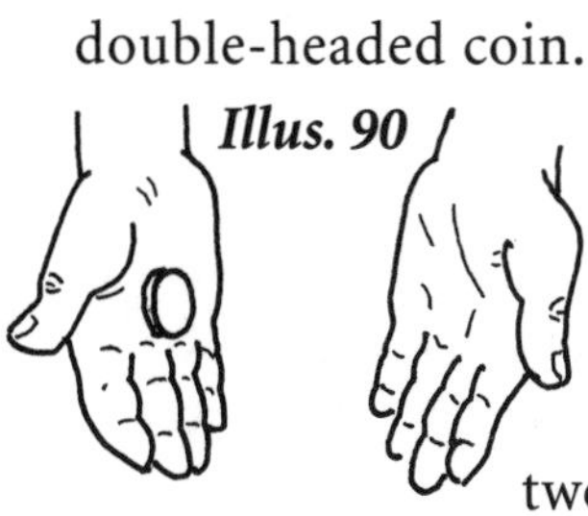

Illus. 90

Hold the coin, the head side-up, in the palm of your right hand, slightly to the left of the middle of your palm.

Say, "Have you ever seen a two-headed coin?"

Display the coin so that all can see it. Hold both hands palms up, your left hand about 6" from your

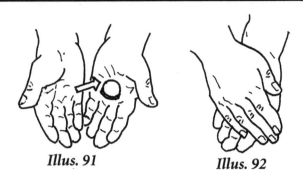

right hand and about 2" lower than your right hand.

Jerk your right hand quickly to the left, letting the coin slide off your right palm and onto your left palm. Obviously, it falls face up (Illus. 91). In the same motion, slap your right hand palm down on your left palm.

This move is done quite rapidly. The illusion is that you've turned the coin over onto your left palm. Lift up your right hand to show that, evidently, the other side of the coin is also a head.

Using the same move, return the coin to your right hand. Show the coin.

Return the coin to your left hand, and then back to your right. You've adequately demonstrated that you have a two-headed coin. You should have a strong ending. Say:

"Many people have offered me a dollar for this fabulous two-headed coin."

Address one of the spectators:

"Would you be willing to pay a dollar for this?"

As you say this, place the coin in your left hand so that the tail side is up. Since you don't want anyone to see the tail side, use the legitimate version of the Easy Vanish move (pages 133 to 135). Hold the coin between thumb and fingers in your right hand, and the coin will naturally turn over as you place it in the palm of your left hand. Close your left fingers over the coin as you withdraw your right hand.

If the spectator says that he would be willing to pay a dollar, open your left hand, saying, "Bad choice." Display the coin on your left palm, showing the tail side. Then lift the coin up and show both sides.

If the spectator says that he wouldn't be willing to pay a dollar say, "Good thinking," and display the coin as above.

Easy Call

To perform this stunt, you must learn a tricky move. The move isn't difficult, however, and the effort will be well rewarded.

Use a half-dollar, although a quarter will do. Flip the coin about 18″ into the air with your right thumb, catch the coin, and then slap the coin onto your left wrist. Illus. 93 shows how to hold the coin when you're about to flip it.

As you flip the coin and slap it onto your wrist a few times, say:

"Wouldn't it be wonderful if you could always tell the way the coin would end up?"

You then call heads or tails, as you flip the coin. Catch the coin, slap it onto your wrist, and, sure enough, you're right.

Illus. 93

Actually, you do not *flip* the coin, although it certainly looks like it. You look at the coin lying in your hand. Suppose that the head side is up. You'll catch it the same way. When you slap the coin onto your wrist, the coin will be turned over. So, as you perform the pseudo-flipping action, you call tails.

Here's the trick move. Hold the coin in your hand as before, but with a slight variation. Your thumb is held back from the coin, and your first finger is above the tip of the coin.

Don't *flip* the coin into the air, but propel it upwards in a

Illus. 94

quick hand movement resembling the regular flipping motion. As you propel the coin upwards, let the side of the coin tick against your first finger. This will give the coin a wobbling motion which looks very much like a regular spin. Naturally, the coin never actually turns over; it returns to your hand with the same side up as when you tossed it.

This move is easy enough to practice, and it shouldn't take you long to get the knack.

Stuck With A Penny

Get a good sport to assist you. Take a penny at the edges and hold it up to your forehead, tail side towards your forehead. Rub it into your forehead, turning the coin in place in a slight circular fashion. The coin will adhere to your forehead. Now say:

"It's easy enough to take the penny away when you use your hands, but otherwise it can be very difficult."

Wrinkle your face up, trying to dislodge the penny. Assume that you aren't successful. Take the penny from your forehead and say to your assistant:

"I wonder if *you* could do it. Okay?"

Again holding the coin at the edges, rub it into your assistant's forehead, *but take the coin away*, dropping your hand to your side. Say:

"Without using your hands, give it a try."

The audience should derive considerable amusement from your assistant's facial contortions as he tries to dislodge the coin.

After he tries for a while, casually begin flipping the penny and catching it. Eventually, he should get the idea and hold his hand to his forehead.

"Good heavens," you might say. "You made it disappear."

Occasionally, your assistant will notice immediately that you did not leave the penny on his forehead. You might say:

"You're right. To tell you the truth, I just didn't trust you with it."

It was once believed that the penny had to be moistened or it wouldn't adhere to the forehead, but this is not true.

Flip-Flop

You may perform this trick using either five half-dollars or five quarters. Half-dollars are better because they're easier for spectators to see. Not many people carry half-dollars, however, so if you're going to borrow the coins, use quarters.

Place the five coins on your left so that they overlap.

Heads and tails should alternate. Say,

"Heads and tails intermixed. Let's see what we can do about that."

Meticulously push the coins into a stack with your right fingers and thumb. Hold the coins at the ends of your fingers and thumb as you lift the coins a few inches above your left hand.

You're now going to drop the coins one at a time onto your left palm. Assume for a moment that the coins are heads up, tails up, heads up, tails up, heads up. When you drop the first one, you will release pressure from both fingers and thumb simultaneously; the coin will fall directly into your left hand, still heads up. With the second coin, however, you will release only the thumb. This will cause the coin to pivot off the fingers and turn over, also landing heads up. The third coin is dropped regularly, the fourth caused to turn over, and the last dropped regularly.

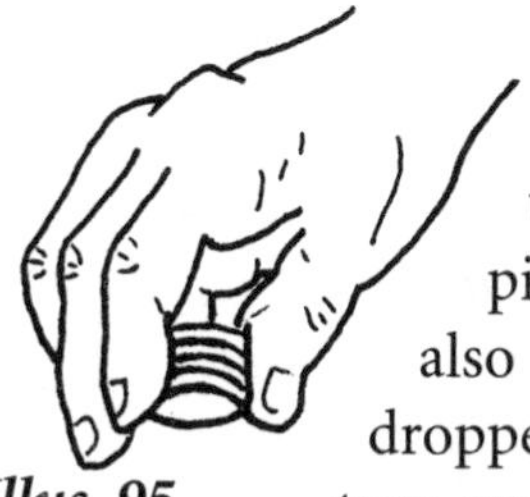

Illus. 95

Show that all the coins are now heads up. The stunt may be repeated.

It isn't easy learning how to drop the coins properly. First, you'll have to determine the correct distance separating your left and right hands. Second, you must figure out how you lessen the thumb pressure so that the coin will pivot off your right fingers and turn over; you must develop a certain "touch." The solution is practice!

Quick Transpo

This trick is fast and effective. A coin held under one hand magically moves under the other hand. Two versions of this trick appear in the book. Quick Transpo is somewhat easier, and it's done standing up. The other, Hand to Hand, follows.

Flip a coin (any size) into the air a few times to keep spectators from focusing on the key move. Hold both hands out and palms up, displaying the coin in the right hand about ½" from the ends of the fingers.

Simultaneously slap your two hands against your stomach, tossing the coin from the right hand so that it lands under the left. Because of the simultaneous movement of the hands, the coin arrives just before the left hand smacks against your stomach.

Rub your right hand against your stomach vigorously, as though rubbing the coin away. Removing your right hand from your stomach and show that it is empty. Turn over your left hand, letting the coin drop into it. Display the coin.

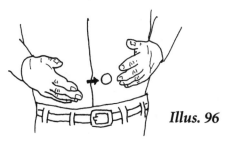

Illus. 96

Don't hesitate to try this trick. There's a good chance that you will succeed in a good throw on your first attempt. You'll get the knack in less than five minutes.

Hand To Hand

This is a slightly more difficult version of Quick Transpo. You'll show a coin in each hand, yet when you slap the coins down on the table, both will end up in the same hand.

Both hands are placed palms up on the table, a coin resting on each hand. The coin in your right hand lies on the right side of the hand, above the thumb and below your first finger, while the coin in your left hand is resting on the second joints of the fingers. The positioning is important, as you're about to toss the coin from the right hand to the left hand, and you don't want a telltale clink. Also, placing the coin on the right side of the right hand makes it easier to throw the coin.

The two hands should be separated by a few inches

more than the width of two hands, or about a foot.

With a quick movement, turn both hands over and inward, smacking them palms down on the table. As you do so, toss the coin from the right hand so that the coin lands under the descending left hand.

The technique of the throw is a bit tricky. As the proper method is described please remember that the entire move takes only a fraction of a second. Raise both hands about 2″ above the table before turning them inward and slapping them down. The coin is tossed as the palms face each other. The coin is slapped down, along with the other coin, with the left hand. Meanwhile, the right hand also smacks the table, right next to the left hand. Keep in mind that you must *throw* the coin from the right hand.

To end the trick, make a circular motion on the table with your right hand; then turn your right hand over and move it aside, showing that the coin has vanished. Lift your left hand, revealing both coins.

When done properly, the passage of the coin is absolutely invisible. About ten minutes of practice should do it.

The position of the coin in each hand has been emphasized. The trick can also be performed with both coins on the palms and both coins on the fingers.

Experiment to find which method works best for you. The trick can be performed with any size of coin, up to a coin the size of a quarter.

Once you develop the proper timing, you can perform the trick with any small object—dice, poker chips, etc.

Coins And Cards

Every experienced coin magician performs a version of this trick. Coins mysteriously pass up through a table, appearing under a playing card or under a piece of cardboard.

Most versions call for considerable skill and sly moves, requiring countless hours of practice. This variation is very easy, yet completely deceptive.

Required are four pennies that look alike and two playing cards—preferably poker-size, because these cards are wider than "normal" cards. You can perform this trick on a bare table or on a table with a covering on which a coin will slide easily. The critical move involves sneakily sliding a coin, so a nubby tablecloth will make a proper presentation impossible. If need be, set a large magazine or a file folder on the table.

Lay out four pennies in a square. The pennies should be about six inches apart. Hold the two cards face down, one in each hand.

Set the card in your *right* hand on top of the upper-left penny, retaining your grip on the card. You explain:

"For this experiment to work, we must get the precisely correct magical combination. We can cover a coin with one card, or we can cover it with two."

Set the card in the left hand on top of the other card, retaining your grip on the card.

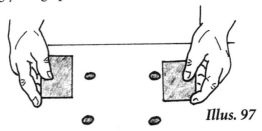

Illus. 97

Slide the card in your right hand to the right, covering the upper-right coin, still retaining your grip on the card.

"Cover two pennies separately…"

Set the card in your left hand on top of the other card, again keeping your grip.

"…or cover one with two cards."

Slide the card in your right hand down to cover the lower-right coin, keeping your grip, and say:

"Cover two pennies separately…"

As before, set the left-hand card on top, retaining your grip, and say:

"…or cover one with two cards."

Slide the card in your *left* hand to the left, covering the lower-left coin. The back of your middle fingers of your left hand, at the knuckle below the fingernails, should be resting on the penny.

"Cover two pennies separately…"

Set the card in your right hand on top, keeping your grip on it.

"…or cover one with two cards."

Now for the key move. Slide your left hand up to cover the upper-left penny with the card. Along with it, slide the penny which is resting under your fingers.

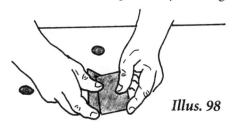

Illus. 98

A coin is being slid forward under the card.

Let go of the card. Two pennies are now resting under it. As soon as the upward movement of the card in your left hand leaves enough room, drop the card in your right hand, presumably covering the lower-left coin.

As you perform the upward movement of the left hand, say:

"Cover two pennies separately…"

You have now dropped both cards.

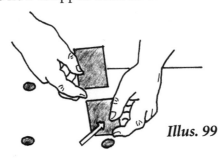

Illus. 99

"That's it!" you declare. "The right combination."

All of the above is down quite rapidly, without pause.

Casually draw back your left hand and let that hand fall into your lap. At the same time, pick up the upper-right coin in your right hand. Hold it up, and announce:

"Let's try this one first."

Bring the coin under the table and tap the underside of the table with your second finger. Try to tap with the end of the fingernail to provide a somewhat metallic sound. Later you'll be tapping *without* a coin, so this sound must be repeated each time.

As you bring your right hand back, toss the penny into your left hand, where it lies on the fingers. Without pausing, bring the right hand out. Reach towards the upper-left card with your palm up. The idea is to show that your hand is empty (without being too obvious). Lift the card off the two pennies.

"Good! It worked."

As you say this, bring the card back to your left hand, which takes it slightly below table level. Under the card, of course, you're holding a penny with your left fingers.

Immediately move your right hand to the two coins, and pick them up and hold them in the air. As you place the card and coin (that are in your left hand) down in the upper-left position, rattle the coins in your right hand, and say:

"Two pennies."

Your left hand now withdraws to the relaxed position on your lap. Your right hand drops the two coins onto the back of the card you just placed down.

The rattling of the coins in your right hand misdirects the spectators' attention from your placement of the card with the coin underneath.

With your right hand, pick up the penny in the lower-right corner, and say:

"Now we'll try this one."

Take the coin under the table, tap, toss it into your left hand, and bring out your empty right hand. Move your right hand palm up to the card in the upper-left corner. Tilt the card so that the pennies on top slide off. Now move the card away, showing that another penny has passed through the table. As before, your right hand moves back and places the card in the left hand, which holds a penny underneath.

Promptly move your right hand forward, pick up the three pennies on the table, and hold them in the air. As you place the card and penny down in the upper-left position, rattle the coins, and say:

"Three pennies."

Drop the pennies on top of the card you just placed down.

The position of the objects on the table should be as follows: In the upper-left corner, you have a card with one penny under it and three pennies on top of it. In the lower-left corner is a card with no coin under it.

Here is the swindle. Place the cupped left hand a few inches below the table, directly behind the card in the lower-left corner. With fingers on top and thumb at the back, slide the card slightly off the table. As soon as the edge of the card clears the table, with your thumb lift the end of the card about 1″. Perform a sweeping motion towards yourself, apparently sweeping the penny off the table into your cupped left hand. Close the left hand as though you were now holding the coin.

"And now this one," you say.

Simultaneously perform two actions. Bring your left hand under the table and tap the underside of the table with your second finger, and then turn the card in your right hand face up and toss it to the right of the other card. This will obscure your sneakiness.

Bring your left hand out and reach palm up towards the card in the upper-left corner. Tilt the card, sliding the three pennies off. Lift the card, showing that the last penny has penetrated the table. Turn the card face up and toss it on top of the other face-up card. Show both sides of your hands, and gather up your materials.

Since this is a fast trick, spectators are likely to be quite dazzled. You may well get a request to repeat it. Simply shake your head and say:

"No, I could never get exactly the right combination again."

To learn this trick, go through it slowly, omitting nothing. Every move has its purpose. Leave out one move and the trick may fail.

You'll know that you're ready to perform the trick publicly when you can go through it quickly and without pause. Performed rapidly, this trick has enormous impact as one coin after another passes through the table and under the card.

Practice your patter as you practice the movements.

This trick is an excellent example of the "one-ahead" principle, which is used in quite a few tricks. Such tricks work because the "dirty work" is done before the spectators are ready to look for it.

Classic Coins Through The Table

Here's a version of one of the most famous coin tricks of all. The effect is truly astonishing. Under the most impossible conditions, the performer seems to pass three coins through a solid table.

The key move requires precise timing; this will take considerable practice. But it will be worth it, for this trick can establish your reputation!

Place six quarters and one half-dollar on the table. Place the quarters in two parallel vertical rows of three each. The rows should be several inches apart. At the top of the row on the right, place the fifty-cent piece. From your viewpoint, the coins should be lined up to look like the drawing below.

"We are using seven coins," you explain, "because seven is my lucky number. Sometimes."

Illus. 100

You simultaneously pick up the two rows, the one on the left with the left hand, the one on the right with your right hand. Start at the top of each row and work towards you. With the right hand, pick up the fifty-cent piece first, and place it on top of the upper quarter. Both are placed on top of the second quarter. And all are placed on top of the near quarter. At the conclusion, the coins are held between your thumb and your fingers, your thumb against the fifty-cent piece. Raise the coins so that they're on edge, resting on the table.

Meanwhile, the left hand has picked up the row on the left, starting with the upper quarter. No attempt is made to pile the coins. At the end, they're held in a loose fist. Turn your hand over so that the back of your hand rests on the table.

Slide your right hand forward to the middle of the table. Tap the fifty-cent piece against the wood, and say:

"The table is very solid on top."

Move your right hand under the table. Set the pile of coins on your leg. Take the fifty-cent piece off the pile, reach under to the middle of the table, and tap the underside of the table with the coin. Say:

"And—surprise, surprise—it's also solid under here."

To cover the slight pause when you leave the quarters on your leg, you might laboriously move your body closer to the table, as though you were trying to reach further under the table; then do the tapping.

Immediately after tapping beneath the table, bring your right hand back to the table, holding your hand in a loose fist. Place your hand so that the back of the hand rests on the table. The hands should be separated by a hand's width plus a few inches.

Illus. 101

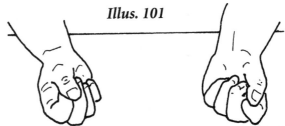

Roll your left hand clockwise, opening it and slapping its coins to the table. Immediately roll your hand back. Your hand is still open so that all can see that it is empty. Say:

"Three coins in this hand."

Turn your left hand over and gather up the three

quarters with your fingers. The hand is back up. The coins are resting on the table, loosely held between the tips of your fingers and the heel of your palm.

Here's the trick move. Two things take place simultaneously: Your left hand lets go of its coins and then rolls counterclockwise as it slaps the fifty-cent piece on top of the three quarters. Immediately roll your right hand back, still open, and say:

"And four coins in this hand."

Pick up the coins with your right hand, holding the coins in a loose fist. As you do so, say:

"A total of seven…perhaps my lucky number."

Bring your right hand under the table. Pick up the coins off your leg, adding them to the ones already in your right hand. As before, move your body closer to the table to cover the brief pause. Bring your right hand with its coins to the middle of the underside of the table.

Slide your left hand to the middle of the table. Turn your hand over and slap it palm down on the table. At the same time, shake your right hand so that the coins jingle. Turn over your left hand, showing that it's empty, and that there are no coins on the table. Bring your right hand from under the table, in a loose fist. Turn your hand over and spread the seven coins out on the table.

Say:

"It worked! Seven is my lucky number."

One reason that this trick works so well is that fifty-cent piece in your right hand. After you've slapped the fifty-cent piece on top of the three quarters on the table, spectators make an assumption that you were holding a fifty-cent piece and three quarters in your right hand, and since there are three quarters and a fifty-cent piece on the table, these must be the same coins you held in your right hand.

The basic move must be practiced until you even fool yourself. To get the timing just right—rolling the left hand out of the way just as your right hand is slapping down the fifty-cent piece—practice the first *without* coins. When you do add the coins, the move will be much easier to perform.

Remember that you're *not* performing a trick move. Do not tense up. Some performers get anxious just before performing a move, and this nervousness serves as a virtual announcement that something tricky is coming. The idea is that you are just showing the coins held by each hand; try to treat it as casually as that.

Don't repeat this trick for the same audience. Consider the requests to repeat the trick as a form of applause. Take a bow and proceed to another trick.

In your patter, don't mention that you are going to try to pass coins through the table; there's no need to put the spectators on guard.

The real key to proper performance of this trick is confidence. If you practice until the moves are automatic, you will have that confidence.

Leg Work

For this trick, the Combined Vanish works best. See pages 135 to 136.

Place your left foot on a chair. Or, if you have an excellent sense of balance, you could raise your knee in the air. Another possibility is to be seated in a chair.

Place a coin—preferably a penny—on your raised left leg near the knee, and another several inches nearer your torso.

Place the back of your open left hand on top of the nearer coin (the one closer to your torso).

Pick up the other coin and pretend to place it in your left hand, using the Combined Vanish (or one of the other vanishes). As you move your right hand away, let the coin fall onto your cupped fingers, so that you will be able to pick up the other coin between your first finger and thumb.

Raise your closed left hand to your mouth, and blow

into your left fist. *At precisely the same time*, pick up the other coin with the first finger and thumb of your right hand.

Hold both hands in front of you in two fists, separated by a foot or so. Revolve both hands slowly several times, and then open them, showing that both coins are in your right hand.

As you perform this trick, you might want to say:

"Like people, coins are sometimes attracted to each other. Here we have two coins, complete strangers, as far as I know."

By this time, you should be ready to show the two coins in your right hand.

"But look. Apparently, there was real magnetism between them."

This trick shouldn't be done speedily. Strive for smoothness and naturalness. The moves should flow. When the moves become automatic, you can perform several repetitions without fear of discovery.

Why does this trick work? Blowing into the left fist while picking up the coin with the right hand tends to confuse spectators. They simply can't follow what you're doing.

Reappearances

Making a Coin Reappear

For the most part, every time a coin disappears, it must also reappear. It doesn't much matter *where* it reappears, but it better show up and soon. Even the dullest observer will eventually figure out that if the coin is not in one hand, it just might be in the other. So after you cause a coin to vanish, bring it back. Produce it from someone's ear, from behind your knee, from your pants pocket, whatever. Keep this in mind while studying the following reappearances.

It's a Toss-Up

You have very cleverly pretended to place a coin in your left hand, whereas it remained in your right hand. Your eyes are locked onto your left hand. Suddenly you throw the invisible coin high into the air. Follow its progress with your eyes as it moves toward the ceiling and then descends. Reach out and catch it in your right hand, and then show it at your right fingertips.

Good Catch

Again the left hand is empty, though everyone thinks it contains a coin. The coin is actually palmed in the right hand, which is hanging at your side. Say a magic word or two and then show everyone that the coin has disappeared from the left hand. Suddenly stare off to your left.

"What's that?" you blurt out.

Reach out your left hand and grab the invisible coin that you've been staring at.

Hold your right hand out palm up, but tilted so that the audience cannot see the palm. Bring the left hand above the right a few inches and open the fingers, dropping the invisible coin into your right palm. Immediately bounce the coin on the right palm a few times and then hold it up at the right fingertips.

From Ear to Ear

You seem to have placed the coin into the left hand, but actually have retained it in the right hand. Now you apparently stick the coin into one ear, and then pull it out of the other.

There are many techniques that can be used, but here's one that works well. Let's say that Peter is standing, facing the group. You move behind him, and also face the group. Your left hand evidently holds the coin between the thumb and the fingertips. The back of the hand is toward the group. Reach over so that the left hand almost touches his right ear (Illus. 102). Pull your thumb back as you push the fingers forward, creating the illusion that you're pushing something into the ear.

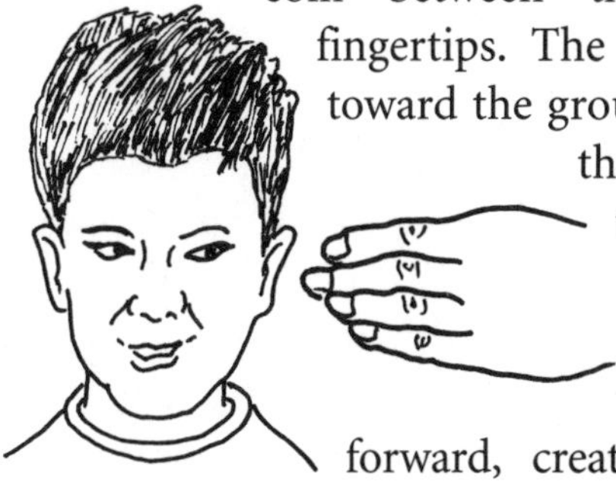

Illus. 102

Immediately bring your right hand close to his left ear, with the back of the hand toward the group. The coin is held between the thumb and finger-tips, but make sure the coin does not project beyond your fingertips.

Now perform an action that is almost the reverse of what you did with the other ear. Draw your fingers back while pushing the coin forward with your thumb (Illus. 103). The coin comes into sight, as though withdrawn from the ear.

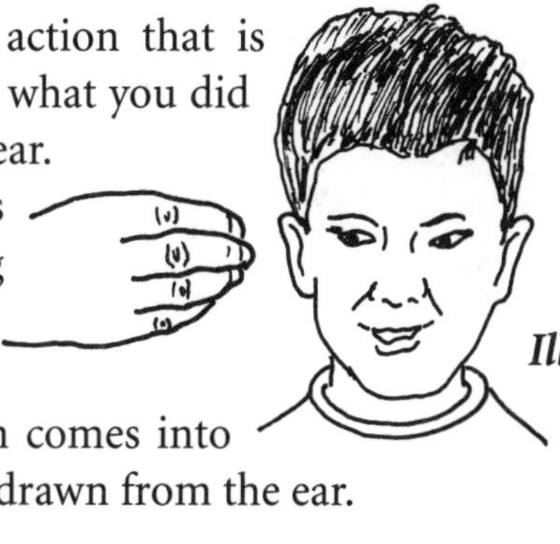

Illus. 103

Hold the coin up for a moment, displaying it, and then bounce it on your palm a few times so that all can see that it actually is the coin.

"Oh, Here It Is!"

Evidently you placed a coin into your left hand; actually, you retained it in your right. Your right hand is closed, except for the first finger, which is extended. Tap the back of the left hand with this extended first finger. Turn your left hand over and open it, showing that the coin is gone. Meanwhile, drop your cupped hand to your side.

Say, "Oh, here it is!" Reach into the air with your left hand and apparently grasp a coin, closing the hand. But when you open the hand, no coin is there.

Staring at the empty hand, you're puzzled. "I guess not."

With the left first finger, point upward and to the right. "There it is!" you declare, reaching out with your right hand and producing the coin at your fingertips.

In Your Ear

Again, with the left hand you reach into the air for a coin, saying, "Here it is!" or "I've got it!"

But, alas, you're wrong. You search the air and then

notice Billy. Reaching for his left ear with your right hand, you discover that the coin was there all along.

Slap 1

As usual, in the next two reappearances, the coin is presumed to be in the left hand, but is actually in the right.

Your left hand is closed. Turn the hand palm down. Open it as you slap the palm against the top of your right leg.

At the same time, bring your right hand palm up beneath the leg.

Turn your left hand over, showing that the hand is empty and that no coin rests on the leg. Then bring the palm-up right hand out, showing that the coin has passed through the leg.

Slap 2

As above, your left hand is closed. Open it as you slap it against the left side of the left leg. Promptly slap the right hand against the right side of the right leg, opening the hand and pushing the coin against the leg.

Turn both hands palm outward, showing that the coin has passed through both legs and, in my case, the considerable space between.

Double Cross

The next three or four moves can be combined to form a powerful mini-routine, and any one of them can be performed separately to good effect.

The sleight in Double Cross is not difficult, but it does require perfect timing, so a fair amount of practice is necessary.

Hold a large coin between the first and second fingers of your right hand, as shown in Illus. 104. The left hand is held in a palm-down fist.

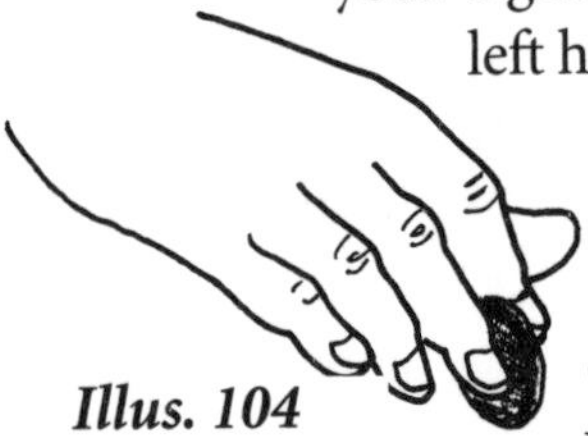

Illus. 104

"This experiment depends upon magic X's," you say. "First, we put X-traordinary X's on my X-cellent X-tremity here." Indicate your left hand. Rapidly move the coin back and forth across the back of the hand, forming an X each time.

Next, draw the right hand back and up several inches. As you do so, curl in all your fingers, so that the coin can be grasped at the base of the thumb and first finger. Immediately extend all the fingers of the right hand (Illus. 105). In the same motion, make a darting move-ment toward the left hand, stop-

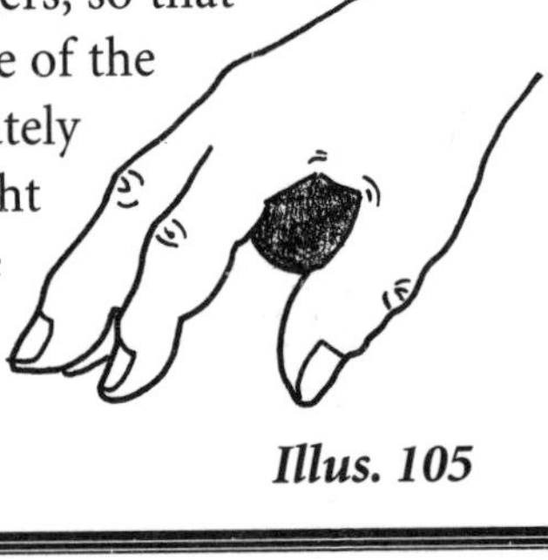

Illus. 105

ping when the tips of the right fingers are gently resting on the back of the left hand (Illus. 106).

You are now going to turn the left hand palm up and lightly draw a few X's across it with the outstretched fingers of the right hand. The first line of the first X will run diagonally, as shown in Illus. 107. But while drawing that first line, a great deal happens:

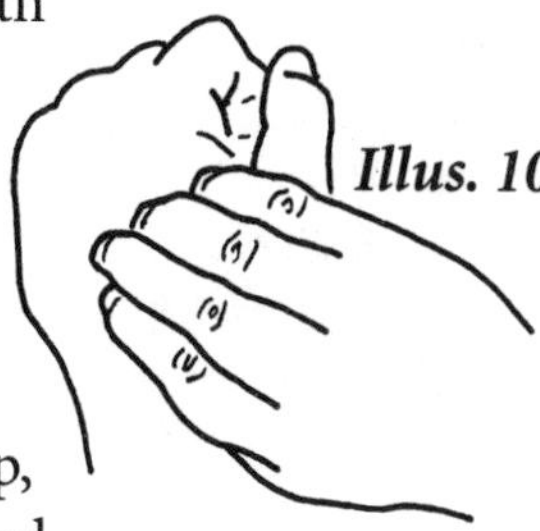

Illus. 106

(1) The left hand is almost palm up, and you're still turning it. Open the hand slightly. This is completely concealed by the right hand.

(2) As the right hand starts drawing the first line of an X, you let the right thumb relax its grip on the coin, which drops into the palm of the left hand.

(3) Immediately close the left hand again.

Illus. 107

(4) You complete the first line of the X. Then you add the other line, and throw in at least two more X's.

While performing this maneuver, say, "And, of course, we must cross the palm a few times."

Next, turn the left hand palm down again and make a few X's with the right fingers across its back. "A few X-tra X's should do it."

With the right hand, make a magical wave at the left hand. Slowly turn the left hand over and show that the coin has penetrated the hand.

Note: *The transfer of the coin from the right to the left hand takes only a fraction of a second. Done properly, the entire move is covered by the back of the right hand. Even when the timing is a tad off, plenty of misdirection is provided by the snappy crossing movements.*

Slap Through the Leg

Let's assume that you've pretended to place a coin in your left hand in one of the vanishes. Do not immediately show the left hand empty. Instead, place your right hand under your right leg and slap the top of that leg with your right hand from behind the leg.

Another version is to slap your left hand against the side of your left leg, then instantly slap your right leg and display the coin at your fingertips, showing that it has penetrated both legs.

If you have performed the French Drop (pags 130 to 132), pretending to take the coin with the *right* hand, simply reverse the hands and proceed as described.

From a Spectator's Ear

Suppose that you've performed the French Drop (pages 130 to 132). You've presumably taken the coin with your right hand, whereas it is actually in the left. Raise your right hand, held in a loose fist, above shoulder level, (as though you were holding the coin up), letting your left hand drop naturally to your side. Then snap the fingersof the right hand. Turn the palm towards the audience, showing that your right hand is empty.

Produce the coin from a spectator's ear. Simply reach towards the spectator's ear with your cupped left hand, the back of your hand towards the spectators. When you are about an inch or so from the spectator's ear, slide the coin to your fingertips with your thumb, and almost touch the ear with the coin. Instantly, push the coin into sight as you pull the hand away from the ear.

Another way to show that the coin has vanished is to drop the right hand to belt level and make an upward tossing movement, as though throwing the coin into the air. You can then produce the coin from the spectator's ear.

Pass Through the Head

This reappearance may be used with any vanish.

Suppose that you've pretended to place a coin in your left hand, whereas it is actually in your right hand.

Approach a spectator. Reach out with your left hand, back of the hand towards the audience, pretending to hold the coin between your thumb and fingertips. Lightly push your fingers against the side of his or her head, above the ear.

Meanwhile, you have let the coin drop onto the fingers of the right hand. Reach out with your right hand, its back to the spectators, so that they can't see that you hold the coin between fingers and thumb. Immediately after you have pushed against the side of the spectator's head with your left hand, produce the coin at your fingertips from the corresponding spot at the other side of the subject's head, using your right hand.

Cough It Up

This reappearance provides a little drama and a touch of humor. Before performing the sleight, bend over so that people can see the top of your head. Touch the middle of your head, saying:

"I don't know if you can see it from there, but I have a little hole in the top of my head. Yes, people are right about me, but it does come in handy now and then."

Perform your choice of vanish, then bring the empty hand, lightly closed as if you are holding the coin, above your head. Open your fingers as you slap the top of your head. *Immediately*, bring the hand holding the coin to your mouth as if to cover a cough, and let your left hand drop to waist level. Cough, and let the coin fall from the hand at your mouth, catching it in the hand at your waist. This trick usually gets a laugh, and always delights children.

You may wish to indicate the hole in the top of your head after performing the vanish. As you explain about the hole, simply touch the middle of your pate with the forefinger of the hand that holds the coin, holding the coin loosely cupped against your palm with the rest of your fingers. While less direct, this can serve to demonstrate that the hand is apparently empty, and you can then proceed to complete the trick as above.

Catch as Catch Can

This excellent method of retrieving a vanished coin is deceptively easy to perform. The timing must be precise, however. Spend as much time practicing this as you would spend on a difficult sleight.

Using any vanish, pretend to place a coin in the left hand. The coin must be held in the palm of the right hand. The left hand is closed; the right hand holds a coin in the palm. Raise both hands to head level, backs of the hands to the spectators. The fingers of the right hand should be spread. Don't worry about the coin; it will stay in the right palm, unseen and quite secure.

Make an upward throwing motion with the left hand, spreading the fingers. Follow the flight of the invisible coin with your eyes, asking, "Where'd it go?"

Make a quarter turn to the left as you do three things: turn the left hand palm towards the audience at waist level, fingers open; drop the right hand to waist level, letting the coin fall onto the left fingers; with the left hand, reach out to the left and grab the invisible coin, saying, "Here!"

Quickly bring the left fist down towards the right hand and, when the left fist is about a foot away from the right hand, make a throwing motion, as though tossing the coin into the right hand. Instantly move the right hand slightly upward, bouncing the coin an inch or so into the air, simulating the catching of the coin, followed by a little bounce. Display the coin at the fingertips, both hands held up, palms toward the audience.

The little bounce when you catch the coin in the right hand is critical. The audience sees the coin hop into view as though it had just arrived. Practice the timing.

Behind The Knee

Very few reappearances can match this one. A coin disappears. You attempt to pull it from your leg using your empty left hand; no luck. You try from the right side of your leg with your empty right hand; still no luck. You try with the left hand again, and there's the coin!

You may use any vanish to (ostensibly) place a coin in your left hand, while retaining the coin in your right hand. The right hand drops casually to your side, as the left hand is shown to be empty.

Immediately drop the left hand, palm outward, to slightly behind the left knee, where you grip a little fabric of your trousers between your fingers and thumb. Apparently, you are trying to pull the coin from the fabric. Let the fabric slide through your fingers, showing that your hand is empty. Return the hand to slightly behind the knee.

You have let the coin drop so that it's resting on the fingers of your right hand. With the back of your right hand to the audience, bring your right hand to the rear of the right side of the knee. Again, you are going to grip the fabric of your trousers. Before you do this, pass the coin to the fingers of the left hand. Simply drop the coin off the ends of your right fingers as you grip the fabric.

The coin falls onto the tips of the left fingers, which hold it against the back of the knee.

Pull out the fabric with the right hand, trying to extract the coin. Let the hand slide off, showing that it's empty.

Try again with the left hand. As you pull out the fabric, the coin is held behind it. Gradually, pull the coin out (Illus. 108).

Apparently, you have shown both hands empty, but you've then produced the coin.

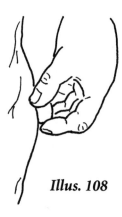

Illus. 108

Seven Cents

You need seven pennies for this trick. This trick can be repeated several times; no particular skill is required.

Show that your hands are empty. Give seven pennies to a spectator. Have him verify that there are only seven.

Take the pennies back and hold them in your cupped left hand. Say to the spectator:

"I'd like you to hold out your left hand so that we can check the count. When I've placed the seventh penny in your hand, I want you to close your hand immediately so that no pennies can escape. Ready?"

Pick up a penny with your right hand, holding it between your second finger and thumb. Your hand should be *palm down* as you place the penny into the palm of the spectator's hand, counting, "One." Place another penny into his hand the same way, making sure that you clink it against the penny already there. As you do so, count, "Two." Continue in the same way with pennies three, four, and five.

Place the sixth penny into his hand in the same way, counting, "Six." Make sure to clink it against one of the coins, *but withdraw your hand, retaining the coin.* Since the back of your hand is to the spectators, no one will see that you still have the coin. Besides, your next move captures everyone's attention.

Immediately, with your left hand, toss the remaining coin into his hand, counting, "Seven." He should close his hand instantly. If he fails to do so, help him with the left hand by placing it beneath his fingers and pushing upward, saying, "Close your hand!"

Quickly show that your left hand is empty and tap his fingers with your left fingers. Bring your right hand under his left and push the coin against it. Bring your hand away, displaying the penny at your fingertips. It's as though you had pulled it through the back of his hand!

Tell the spectator:

"There seems to be a hole in your hand. Let's try it again."

Take the pennies and repeat the trick at least once. Repeating it three times is just about right.

Aspiring magicians have a tendency to feel that the move involved in this trick is much too bold, and that they won't get away with it. At the time you keep the penny, all attention is on the delivery of the seventh coin and the closing of the hand.

The key is to keep a consistent rhythm as you count the coins into the spectator's hand. The sixth coin should be counted out in precisely the same way as the first five.

This is a very difficult trick to practice, since it's difficult to duplicate the actual action by placing coins on a table, for instance. You'll probably have to rehearse with a trusted friend. Don't be surprised if you fool your friend on your first try!

Throwback

Display a coin in your right hand. Point to it with your left hand.

Swing both arms down so that they go slightly behind your back, and then instantly swing them up again, your right hand tossing the coin into the air about two feet or so. Both hands are back to the audience. Your left hand has its first finger extended so that it can point to the coin which has been tossed into the air.

Your right hand catches the coin, and both arms swing down again, going behind your back. Again the coin is tossed into the air and caught by your right hand as your left first finger points.

When your hands swing behind your back the third time, the coin is tossed from your right hand to your left. Both hands come up as before, and the invisible coin is tossed into the air, with your left first finger pointing.

In great puzzlement, look at your empty right hand as

you show its palm to the audience. At the same time, let your left hand drop to your side, fingers loosely curled around the coin. *Immediately*, say, "Ah, there it is!" With your right hand, reach to a spectator's left ear as though to produce the coin. Close your fingers and thumb as though grasping the coin. Then, looking puzzled, show the hand empty. "Wait a minute," you say, as you reach out with your left hand and produce the coin from his right ear.

There are other possible conclusions. You could do Behind the Knee, (pages 177 to 178).

The Magic Circle

A coin is placed in a handkerchief, which is held in the left hand. The coin mysteriously disappears. This is an excellent old trick that would be enormously improved if you could show that the coin is not in your right hand, but you can't

This method gets rid of the coin, enhancing the trick and also providing additional entertainment. For the trick to work, all spectators must be directly in front of you.

Hold your left hand palm up and drape a handkerchief over it. The hand should be at the center of the handkerchief. One corner of the handkerchief should rest on your wrist.

Place a fifty-cent piece in the center of the handkerchief so that you can grip the coin through the fabric
with your left hand, fingers at the front and thumb at
the back. About two-thirds of the coin should be
showing (Illus. 109).

With your right hand, grasp the corner of the handkerchief which is resting on your wrist and bring it
forward over the coin. As the handkerchief covers the
coin, turn your left hand over so that your fingers point
to the floor. Move your right hand away and point to the
coin under the handkerchief, and say:

"Did everyone see the coin?"

Reverse the motions just described, so that the fifty-
cent piece is again on display. Move your left hand from
side to side so that all may see the coin.

"A fifty-cent piece," you declare.

Again cover the coin as you did before the last step.
But, as your right hand reaches its lowest position,
release your grip on the coin, dropping it into your
cupped right fingers (Illus. 110).

As before, point to the presumed coin under the
handkerchief, raising the handkerchief to arm's length
above your head. The coin, of course, is held by the
cupped second, third, and fourth fingers of your right

hand. Casually let your right hand drop to your side.

As you raise the handkerchief above your head, start turning around clockwise. With little shuffles of the feet, turn in a complete circle, yet stay in the same place. Your left hand continues to hold the handkerchief high above

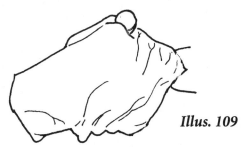

Illus. 109

your head. Throughout the turn, you will talk, saying something like this:

"Have you ever heard of the magic circle? Well, before your very eyes I am making a magic circle right now. There is no extra charge for this feat. I'm happy to do it for you. Who knows? Maybe someday you'll learn to make a magic circle of your own."

By this time, you should be facing the front again. While making your "magic circle," you did something extremely sneaky. When your left side was towards the audience, you dropped the coin into your right trouser pocket. Or, if that pocket wasn't available, you might have tucked it under the top of your trousers or your skirt.

You're still holding the handkerchief (and supposedly, the coin) at arm's length above your head. Reach up

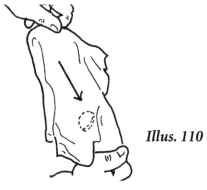

Illus. 110

with your right hand and take a corner of the handkerchief between your first and second fingers. Let go with the left hand and let the handkerchief fall, held only at the corner by the right fingers. This is a very showy climax.

You're holding one corner of the handkerchief between two fingers of your right hand. Switch the grip, so that you're holding it between your thumb and first finger. Take an adjacent corner between the thumb and first finger of your left hand and spread the handkerchief between the hands, palms to the audience. Reverse the position of your hands, showing the other side of the handkerchief. Give the handkerchief to your audience for them to examine and show both sides of both hands.

Say, "Thank goodness the magic circle worked!"

While you make your magic circle, all attention is on the handkerchief you are holding aloft. This misdirection of the audience's attention is perfect for ditching the coin.

MAGIC TRICKS

Hand Tricks

Disjointed Digit

This trick works particularly well for children, but most adults are also amused by it. Apparently you remove the first finger of your right hand.

"I have some amazing feats for you. Actually, they're not feats, but hands. Just watch these magical fingers."

Wiggle your fingers, demonstrating their amazing flexibility. Position your left hand so that your fingers point down and the back of your hand is towards the spectators. Tuck your left thumb into your left palm. Bring your left hand in front of your right. Bend in the first finger of your right hand. Your left hand, of course, conceals this. Rest your left hand on the back of your right hand, fingers still down.

Illus. 111

The broken outline shows the position of your left hand.

Say, "Watch carefully."

Twist your left hand upwards, raising the second, third, and fourth fingers. The first finger stays down, hiding the fact that your left thumb is bent inward. The illusion is that your

188

left thumb is the outer joint of your right first finger.

Move your thumb along the surface of your right second finger several times, demonstrating that the outer joint of your right first finger is separated from

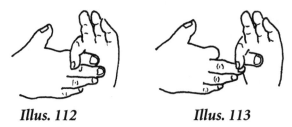

Illus. 112   **Illus. 113**

the rest of your finger. Then, extend your left fingers again and straighten out your right first finger, grasping it in your left hand. Twist your right hand several times in a semicircle, "repairing" your finger. Hold up your right first finger and waggle it, showing that it's fully restored.

Incredible Shrinking Finger

You not only can remove one of your fingers, but you can also shrink one.

Hold up your left hand straight, back of your hand to the onlookers. Grip the little finger of your left hand with your right hand. The first finger and thumb of

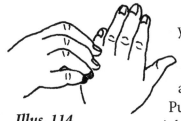

Illus. 114

your right hand hold the top knuckle. The remaining fingers of your right hand are cupped outwards.

Push downwards with your right thumb and first finger, holding the top of your finger straight. At the same time, however, bend the lower knuckle of your little finger outwards. You're concealing this bend with your second, third, and fourth right fingers.

Very slowly, push your little finger down, laboriously reducing its size. The illusion is quite realistic, since the tip of your finger remains pointing upward, and the finger slides down next to straight, extended fingers.

Agonize as you pull your finger back up. Repeat the reduction. You might even try it a third time. Finally, pull your finger back up, grasp it with your right hand, and rub the finger vigorously. Then show your left hand, moving all the fingers to show that everything is as it should be.

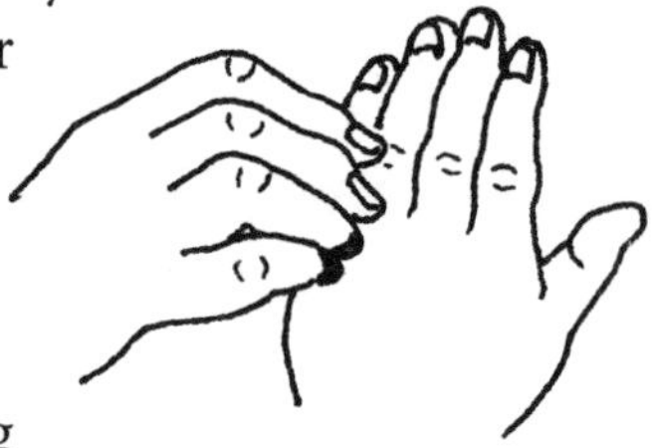

Illus. 115

Go Away

Some readers may remember this stunt from their childhood. It's amusing to those who've seen it before, and amazing to those who haven't.

You should be seated at a table. Tear off two bits of paper from a napkin, a tissue, or a paper towel. Moisten the bits of paper and stick one on the fingernail of each of your first fingers.

Place the tips of your first fingers on the edge of the table. Bouncing the two fingers rhythmically, you chant line one: "Two little birds sitting on a hill…"

Bounce the right finger as you say, "One named Jack, …"

Bounce the left finger as you say, "One named Jill."

"Go away, Jack." As you say this, swing your right hand up and past your head. During the swing up, fold in your first finger and extend your second finger. Instantly bring the hand down to the table, displaying the second finger.

Immediately say, "Go away, Jill." Perform the same switching action with your left hand. No one has time to observe what you actually did, because you proceed without hesitation to the next step.

Swing up your right hand again, and switch fingers again as you say, "Come back, Jack." Instantly do the same with your left hand, saying, "Come back, Jill."

Do not repeat the stunt.

The key is to perform the stunt *rapidly*. Once you start, the whole sequence should last no more than ten seconds. A few minutes' practice should give you complete mastery.

Here's the rhyme in one piece:

Two little birds, sitting on a hill,
One named Jack, one named Jill.
Go away, Jack. Go away, Jill.
Come back, Jack. Come back, Jill.

Let's Go To The Hop!

Since the principle here is the same as that of Go Away (see previous trick), avoid doing both tricks for the same group at the same time.

Use any one of the following: a colored rubber band wound around your finger several times; an address label, moistened and attached to your finger; a scrap of thin paper (napkin, tissue), moistened and stuck on your finger; or a plastic bandage.

Use the second finger of your right hand. Let's assume you've wound a colored plastic bandage around your second finger. Extend the first two fingers of your right hand. Make sure that the other fingers are well folded in, and that your thumb is out of sight (Illus. 116).

Hold out your left hand palm up; your right hand should be about 8" (20 cm) above. Bring down your right hand to your left hand, displaying briefly the extended two fingers of your right hand. Leave your fingers there for only a fraction of a second—just long enough for onlookers to see them; then bring up your right hand to its original position. As you bring your right hand down again to display your fingers, fold in your first finger and extend your third finger (Illus. 117).

Illus. 116

"Watch it hop!" you say. Bring up your right hand again, and, as you bring it down, switch fingers once more. Repeat the switch several times rapidly. The illusion is that the label (or bandage) is hopping back and forth between your fingers.

Illus.117

Revolving Wrist

This brief, extraordinary stunt is a real reputation-maker. Apparently, you're either magical or double-jointed, for you can turn your hand completely around in a manner that's physically impossible.

To start, you must be wearing a suit jacket or sport

coat, or the equivalent. For example, a sweater with long, loose sleeves will do.

Kneel down, press your hand against the floor, and turn your hand 360 degrees. It's quite impossible, and it looks ridiculous. When people see you do it, they'll either laugh or gasp.

The secret is quite simple, however, and you'll accomplish the feat easily on your first try. "Ladies and gentlemen," you might say, "I've been practicing magic for some time. As a result, I've gained astonishing control over various parts of my body. Let me show you." Kneel down. Grasp your right sleeve with your left hand so that you can hold the sleeve in place while performing your maneuver. Turn your right hand palm-up and twist that hand counterclockwise as far as you can. Rest the back of your right hand on the floor (Illus. 118).

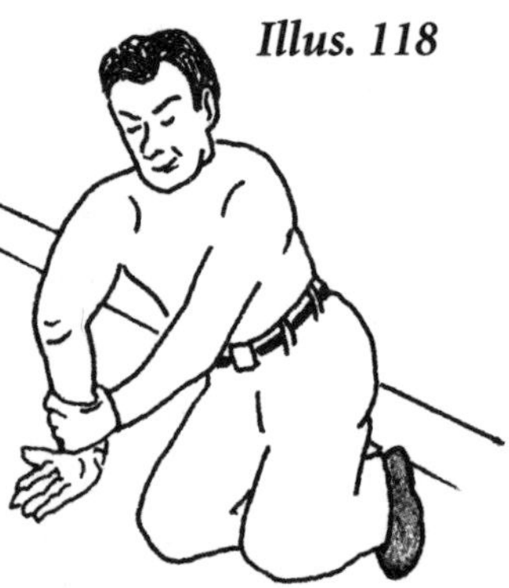

Illus. 118

You should be feeling some strain in your arm and wrist, but that sensation will be quite brief, for you'll begin the maneuver immediately. Very slowly rotate your arm clockwise, holding the sleeve so that it stays steady.

Your hand, still pressed against the floor, also turns clockwise, of course. You strain a bit at the end to bring your hand to precisely the position it was in at the beginning. Illus. 119 shows your hand at various phases of the move.

Leave your hand in its final position for a few seconds, and then stand up, shaking your hand and arm.

Your audience asks, "How did you do that?" Don't tell them. If you do, you'll turn an astonishing feat into an insignificant little trick. *Don't repeat this trick*—at least not during that

Illus. 119

performance. Retrospectively, spectators assume that you started with your hand palm-down; don't destroy that illusion! The secret isn't well known, so keep it that way.

Knife Tricks

Sticky Knife #1

This *old* stunt is a perfect introduction to Sticky Knife #2 (see next trick). Ancient it might be, but this golden oldie will still provide oodles of fun.

Hold a table knife on your left palm with your left thumb (Illus. 120). Grip your left wrist with your right hand. Turn over your left hand, revolving your left hand in your right hand, which remains still. As you do this, turn your hand downward, so that your left fingers point towards the floor. At the same time, extend your right first finger so that it holds the knife. Now stick out your left thumb, so that all can see it (Illus. 121).

Move your hands together, back and forth. The knife mysteriously clings to the palm of your left hand. Stop the movement and then precisely reverse the movements you performed when turning over your left hand. First, bring your left thumb onto the knife. Then revolve your left hand, palm up, as you return your right first finger to the side of your wrist.

Repeat the trick, if you wish. You might even consider teaching it to interested spectators. The next knife suspension, however, you won't teach; it's much too good a trick.

Illus. 120   **Illus. 121**

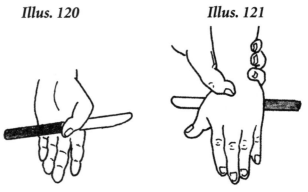

Sticky Knife #2

Hold up a table knife and say, "I'll now glue this to the palm of my hand." You attach the knife to your hands by interlocking your fingers, so that the second finger of your left hand is actually slid into the palm of your right hand, while your remaining fingers interlock alternately. As you interlock your fingers, slide the knife under your left second finger so that it's held secure against your right palm (Illus. 122). Don't perform this procedure in plain sight. If you're sitting at a table, take the knife under the table and attach it to your hands. If you're standing up, simply turn away for a moment while you perform the "dirty work."

Illus. 122

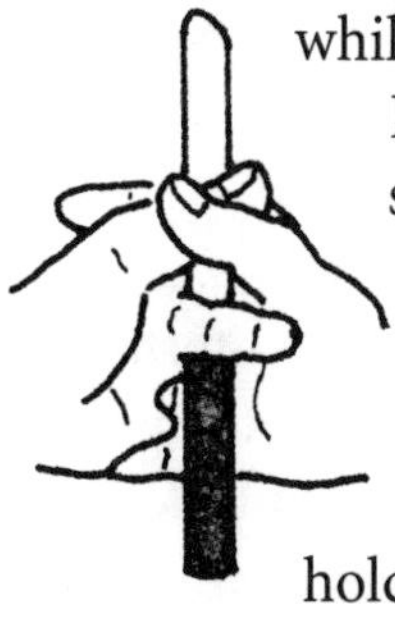

Bring your hands and the knife into sight, the back of your hands towards the spectators, and the knife perpendicular to the floor. Hold your thumbs down so that onlookers will get the impression that your thumbs are holding the knife. Move your hands from side to side. "See? The knife is glued on." If no one comments about your thumbs, say, "You seem skeptical. The thumbs? Not at all." Raise your right thumb about your hand. "See? One thumb." Lower your right thumb and raise your left thumb. "And there's the other thumb."

Move your hands from side to side with your left thumb raised. If no one raises an objection, pretend to hear one. "Both thumbs? Oh, all right!"

Raise the other thumb. What? Your thumbs aren't holding the knife? But how…?

Wave your hands about, moving them backwards and forwards, side to side. Even tilt your hands, bringing them almost level, making sure no one can see your sneaky second finger, the one that's gripping the knife.

Abruptly separate your hands, taking the knife in one. Set down the knife and show both sides of your hands. No stickum, no rubber bands—just sheer magic!

This stunt may also be performed with a pencil, but I find it to be hard on my second finger.

The Levitating Knife

Effect: This is one of those delightfully entertaining impromptu effects that you can nonchalantly present between courses at your next dinner party. Interlock the fingers on both your hands and place them, palms down, on top of a dinner knife. When you raise your hands in front of you, the knife appears to be clinging to them.

At this point, both of your thumbs are hidden behind your fingers and everyone assumes that they are holding the knife against your palms. Tell them that this is not so, and raise your right thumb. They will say that your left thumb is now holding the knife. Move your right thumb back down behind your fingers and raise your left thumb. They will, of course, say that your right thumb is now holding the knife.

Repeat this back and forth several times, and then finally in exasperation raise both your thumbs to show them how wrong they are (Illus. 123). Shake your hands vigorously. The knife will still cling to them. Suddenly, pull your hands apart and let the knife fall to the table. Turn your hands palms up so that your dinner guests can see that they do not conceal anything that could have caused the knife to cling to them. How did you do it?

Presentation: The secret lies in the way you interlocked your fingers. Although no one is about to count your fingers, in reality only nine of them are showing (Illus. 123).

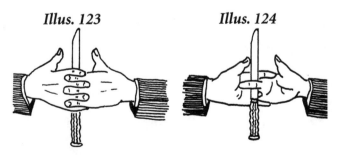

Illus. 123   *Illus. 124*

When you interlock them, do it in such a way that the second finger of the right hand is curled into your palm (Illus. 124). When you pick up the knife, make sure that it goes under this finger, where it will be held in place until you unlock your fingers at the end of the trick.

This is a surprising trick, and one that you should have a lot of fun presenting.

Tricks with Paper

Dippy Die

To perform this trick, you'll have to memorize a bit and practice a little, but no particular skill is required, and the entertainment value is enormous.

A little preparation is required. Prepare a 3 x 5" (7.5 x 13 cm) file card in advance, or use a business card.

In either case, you must take a pen—a marking pen is best—and make little circles on the card, so that the card somewhat resembles a domino. Be sure to color in the circles so that they can be easily seen. On one side, draw two circles, as shown in Illus. 125.

Turn over the card, as though you were turning the page of a book. On this other side, draw five circles, as shown in Illus. 126.

Let's assume that you're sitting around with friends. If

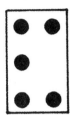

Illus. 125   **Illus. 126**

you're going to use a business card, casually mark the card while chatting, letting the card rest on your tilted left hand (assuming you're right-handed), shielding what you're doing. In a restaurant, as you mark the card, you can rest it on your raised menu. Incidentally, the printing on one side of the business card shouldn't be a problem; just make sure that you mark the printed side with the two dots.

The key to this stunt is the way you hold and turn the card. For clarity, the illustrations will show the use of a file card.

"Did you ever play card craps?" you ask, keeping your card out of sight. Your friends are likely to answer no.

"Me neither. Until the other night. I met a stranger in a restaurant, and he asked me that very question. 'Did you every play card craps?' I said, 'No.' He said, 'Nothing to it. I have a magic card that's just like a die. It's a perfectly flat card. On one side is a 1, on the other is a 2, on the other is a 3, on the other is a 4, on the other is a 5, and on the other is a 6.' I said, 'That's impossible.' He said, 'No, that's magic. Here's the way the game goes: We look at both sides of the card. If the two sides total 7, you lose the bet. Then I do it again, doubling the bet. And if I get a 7 this time, you lose...providing I get a 7 with two numbers different from the first ones. If I don't, I lose.' I said, 'You've got a bet,' and I put down some money."

Take out the card and hold it in your left hand, so that the number, from the spectator's view, seems to be 6. (See Illus. 127).

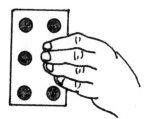

Illus. 127

All the remaining illustrations for this trick will be from the spectators' point of view.

Say, "6 on one side." Bring up your right hand, fingers behind covering the bottom dot and thumb in front (Illus. 128). Quickly rotate your right hand counterclockwise, letting go with your left hand. You're now apparently displaying a 1. Say, "And 1 on this side. 6 and 1 are seven. I gave the man the money."

"I said, 'Now we'll double the bet. Let's see you get a 7

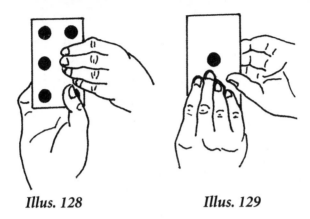

Illus. 128   **Illus. 129**

with two numbers different from the first ones.' And he
did it."

Grip the card with your left hand, thumb on the front
and fingers on the back (Illus. 129). Your fingers should
cover the spot on the left side. Rapidly rotate your left
hand so that the back of your hand is towards the spectators, and the card is turned end for end. As you do so,
let go with your right hand. The spectators are now
looking at 4 dots (Illus. 130).

Say, "4 on one side."

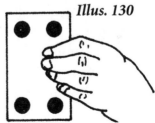

Illus. 130

As before, grip the bottom of
the card with your right fingers on
the back of the card and right
thumb in front. Turn the card so
that the back of your fingers are to

the front. You're apparently displaying 3 dots. Say, "And 3 on this side. 4 and 3 are seven. I gave the man the money."

Without changing your grip, drop your hand to your side as you say, "I told the fellow, 'That's fine, but how about giving me a turn with the card?' He said, 'Okay, I'll give you two tries. Each time double or nothing. So I grabbed that card and went to work."

When you display the numbers for your turn, the handling will be different. Grasp the card in the usual manner with your left hand, (as shown in Illus. 129, page 203). Turn the card end-for-end, displaying an apparent 6 spots. Say, "6 on this side."

Now for the different handling. Turn your left hand so that the card's long side is parallel to the floor. With your right hand, grip the card on the right side, fingers on the back of the card and right thumb in front (Illus. 131). Turn over the card with your right hand. Immediately turn your right hand palm-up so that you display the spots as shown in Illus. 132.

Say, "And 3 on this side. 6 and 3 are nine. I lost again, but I bet one more time."

Revolve your right hand, turning it palm-down. Take the left-hand grip in the usual manner (Illus. 133). Turn the card end-for-end, displaying 4 spots. Say, "4 spots on this side."

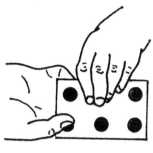

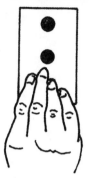

Illus. 131   **Illus. 132**

As before, turn your left hand so that the card's long side is nearly parallel to the floor. Your right hand grips the card on the right side, fingers on the back of the card covering the dot and your right thumb in front. Turn over the card so that you display 1 dot. Say, "Whoops! One dot on this side. 4 and 1 are five. I lost again."

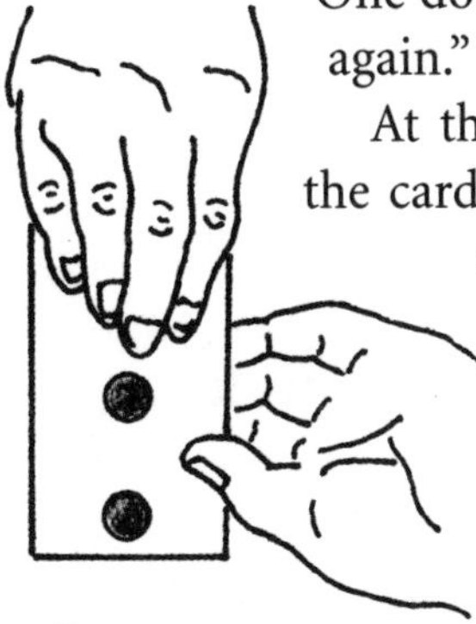

At this point, if you wish, you can tear the card into little pieces, saying, "I was so disgusted I tore up the card and called it quits." Some spectators may be baffled as to how you accomplished this magical feat. With children, I almost always close by tearing up the card.

Illus. 133

Here's the way I prefer to finish:

Drop your hand to your side, saying, "The stranger said, 'Let's have another game. It's my turn with the magic card.' I said, 'Sure. Double or nothing. Only this time, no tricky turns. Just drop the card on the table…and then turn it over on the table.' He said, 'Okay,' and took the card."

Drop the card on the table. "5 dots on this side." Flip the card over. "And 2 dots on this side. 5 and 2 are seven."

Rip the car to shreds. "The moral is, 'Never gamble with strangers.'"

Notes: If you use a business card rather than a file card, you can adequately hide the dots with one or two fingers, rather than three.

The moves aren't really difficult. Mark a card and follow the directions. In short order, the moves will be second nature to you.

The Beelzebub Paper Trick

Effect: Your friends will think that this is a Devil of a trick if you do it well. Pass a length of rope and a stiff piece of paper in the shape of a bell to your audience for examination. Next, have someone thread the bell onto the rope and then have him tie each end of the rope to your wrists (Illus. 134).

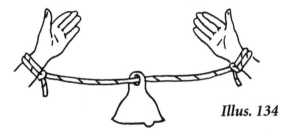

Illus. 134

You can even have him seal the knots with tape. Last, have him drape a large cloth over your arms so that your hands, the rope, and the bell are out of sight. In ten seconds flat, drop the cloth and show that the paper bell has been removed undamaged from the rope and that your hands are still securely tied. The rope and bell may once more be examined.

Materials Needed:
- One piece of rope three feet long
- Two identical paper bells
- A large cloth about three feet square

Preparation: Place one of the paper bells in your shirt pocket under your jacket.

Presentation: Everything occurs as described above up to the point where the cloth is placed over your arms. At this point, raise your arms chest high. Under cover of the cloth, tear the bell off the rope, crumple it up, and slip it into your inside jacket pocket. Remove the other paper bell from your shirt pocket and drop it on the table. Shake the cloth off your arms, and the trick is done. Another version of the trick would be to try secreting the second bell up the sleeve of your jacket instead of in your shirt pocket. This way, you wouldn't have to raise your arms up to your chest.

A Paper Magnet

Effect: "Yes, Ladies and Gentlemen, you heard me correctly: a paper magnet is both a possibility and a fact! Watch closely while I demonstrate this new wonder of science. First, I take this pencil and draw a picture of a magnet on this small piece of cardboard (Illus. 135). Next, I cut a 2-inch piece from this paper straw and place it on the table. To magnetize the paper magnet, I

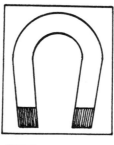

Illus. 135

rub it vigorously back and forth on a piece of cloth to build up a charge of static electricity.

"I now place the magnet on the table just in front of the paper straw. Watch this: As I move the magnet away from the straw, the straw follows it. Did you see that? Here, I'll do it once more before the magnet loses its power. There goes the straw again. It's amazing what new discoveries are made in science every day."

Materials Needed:

- A pencil
- One small piece of cardboard
- A paper straw
- A piece of cloth

Presentation: The cardboard magnet isn't really magnetized. When the performer bends over the table and draws the card away from the straw, he opens his lips slightly and gently blows a stream of air down onto the table just behind the straw (Illus. 136). A little practice will show you just how easy it is to make the piece of straw appear to be following the card across the table. You can also present this as a puzzle and see how long it takes your audience to discover how you make the straw move.

Try not to purse your lips when you blow down on the table, as this can give the secret away. Just part your lips slightly when you blow on the straw. A steady flow

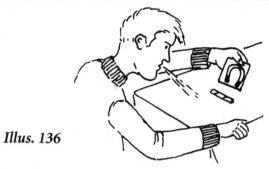

Illus. 136

of chatter and a lot of hand movement will help to distract your audience from seeing how you're really making the straw move.

The Heaven-and-Hell Paper Trick

This is a great bit of magic that can be done with a single sheet of paper. Present the following story to your audience.

"I once heard a story concerning greed that I would like to pass on to you. It seems that two souls confronted St. Peter at the gates of Heaven and asked to come in. St. Peter told them that there was but room for one of them and that they must therefore draw lots to see who was the worthier. St. Peter then took a sheet of paper and folded it once, and then once again, and finally a third time. (Illus. 137-140).

He then tore the folded sheet of paper into two unequal portions (Illus. 141) and was about to speak

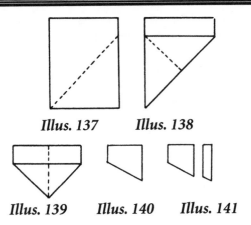

Illus. 137   *Illus. 138*

Illus. 139   *Illus. 140*   *Illus. 141*

when one of the two souls knocked the other aside and reached out and grabbed the larger portion of paper. 'I have the bigger piece,' he shouted. 'I won, let me in!"

"'Quiet,' commanded St. Peter, 'let us see what these lots have to tell us. The smaller piece belongs to this gentleman who has yet to speak. If we open it up, we

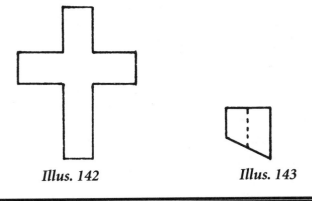

Illus. 142   *Illus. 143*

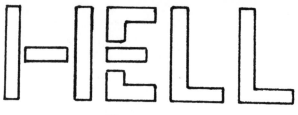

find that it is in the shape of a cross (Illus. 142). Now, let me have the piece that you so rudely took from me. Before we open it up, we will tear it down the middle (Illus. 143). Now, we'll open up the pieces and see what they have to tell you.'

"When the pieces were opened up, the hasty man found that they formed the word HELL (Illus. 144).

"Seeing his fate clearly written before him the man turned to go, but St. Peter bade him enter along with the other man, saying, 'There is always room for one more up here, and I can see from this lesson that greed has been driven out of your heart for good.' I'd say that's a pretty good lesson for all of us."

The Fantastic Fir Tree

Effect: Take five or six sheets of newspaper and roll them into a tight tube while telling your audience a few jokes to keep their attention. At the conclusion of the jokes, turn this tube into a six-foot-high fir tree.

Materials Needed:

• Five or six strips of newspaper twelve inches in width, cut from several double-sheets of newspaper

• A rubber band

Presentation: Take one of the strips and start rolling it up into a cylinder. When you get to the last 5 inches of the strip, overlap another sheet (Illus. 145) and keep on rolling. Do this with each of the remaining sheets until the tube is complete.

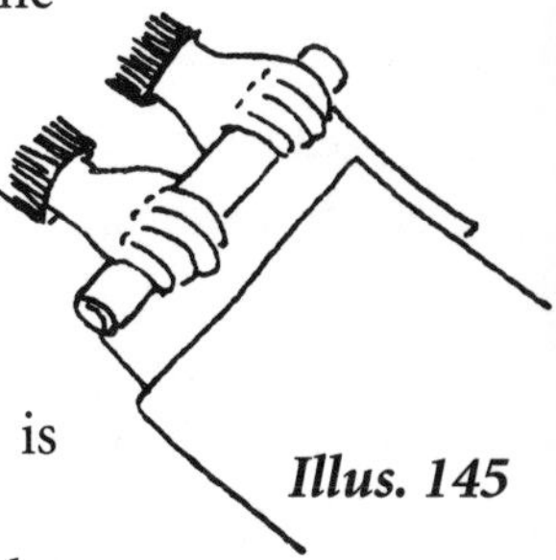

Illus. 145

Snap a rubber band around the tube near the bottom. Flatten out the tube and tear it down the center. Stop about two-thirds of the way down (Illus. 146).

Flatten out the tube on the other side and tear it again the same way (Illus. 147). Bend the four sections of strips down along the sides of the tube (Illus. 148).

Take hold of the tube with one hand, and with the other reach into the center of the tube and take hold of a few of the strips. Gently pull them up and out of the tube. Keep pulling and working the strips upward (Illus. 149).

Illus. 146

You will end
up with a paper
fir tree about five
or six feet high,
depending on
how many strips
of paper you
used to make the
tube.

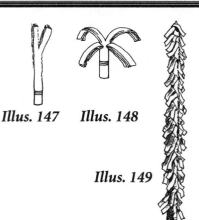

Illus. 147   *Illus. 148*

Illus. 149

Tricks with Rope

String Out #1

Required is a length of string or cord about 4′ (1.2 m) long. Tie the ends in a square knot. Stick your thumbs inside the loop and extend the string. Display the string at about neck level for all to see.

"Now here's a real riddle for you: Do I have a magic neck or a magic string? I'll let you decide."

Without removing your thumbs, swing the looped string over your head so that the string is behind your neck (Illus. 150).

"Now watch carefully."

Quickly bring your hands together and insert your left first finger into the loop just behind your right

Illus. 150

For clarity, the string in all the string tricks is shown as thicker than it actually is.

thumb. Pull to the right with your right thumb and pull to the left with your left first finger. Illus. 151 shows the beginning of this movement. Your left thumb naturally drops out of the loop, but only momentarily. Immediately, and without halting the motion, place your left thumb next to your left first finger and let the thumb take over the pulling motion to the left. Your left first finger will automatically be disengaged from the loop. Snap your thumbs against the inside of the loop as you extend the string forward. The position now is the same as at the beginning. Apparently, you've pulled the string through your neck!

Illus. 151

The entire move is done in a fraction of a second. After you've practiced it a half-dozen times, you'll have mastered it for life.

If you feel like it, you could perform the stunt just one more time.

Note: The trick may be done in other ways. You may, for example, pull the string through a belt loop. Most effective, perhaps, is to place the string around a spectator's arm and then, apparently, pull it right through his arm.

String Out #2

With the same looped string from the previous trick, you can perform another escape.

Hold the string between your two hands, fingers pointed towards yourself (Illus. 152). Bring the right side of the string over the left side, forming a small loop inside the larger loop (Illus. 153). Between your teeth, lightly hold the portion where the strings cross.

Stick your left thumb into the end of the large loop, pulling it fairly tight, so that the smaller loop will be below it. Now, *from below*, stick your right first finger up through the smaller loop. Bring that finger over the right side of the large loop, under the left side, and to your nose. The dark arrow in (Illus. 154) shows the route of your first finger to your nose. Continue holding your right finger to the tip of your nose as you pull the larger loop with your left thumb and release the string from your teeth. The string comes free, apparently passing right through your fingers.

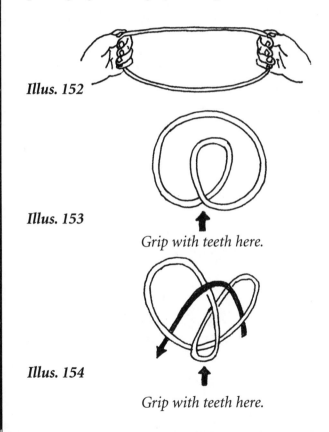

Illus. 152

Illus. 153

Grip with teeth here.

Illus. 154

Grip with teeth here.

No Noose Is Good Noose

You can perform yet another unusual escape trick with that same looped string or cord.

"Here we have an enormous noose," you say, placing the loop over your head. At about the halfway point, cross the loop in front of your face and grip the crossing point between your teeth.

As clearly as you can under these adverse circumstances, say, "But this would be a much more effective hanging device if it were a *double* noose."

Cross the cord back again *the same way*, and place the rest of the loop back over your head. If you originally crossed the right-hand portion on top, it's vital that you recross it on top.

Mumble dramatically and indistinguishably about what a thrilling climax this wonderful trick will have. Grip the string on the right side with your right hand, open your mouth, and quickly pull the string off.

The Sliding Knot

A stage magician cuts a length of rope into two pieces and ties two of the ends together. A spectator holds the loose ends. The magician grasps the knot in the middle and *slides it right off the rope*, and the rope is completely restored!

I've always found this effect to be both amazing and amusing. Here's a version you can do with a pair of scissors and a 3' (1 m) length of string or cord.

Tie the ends of the cord together, forming a loop. Hold this loop between your hands, fingers pointed towards yourself. (See Illus. 152 on page 217 for the proper position.) Now, revolve your left hand, turning the string and forming a double loop. This is what spectators will assume you're doing. But in performance, you're much sneakier. When you form that double loop you give the string an extra half-turn with your left hand. Thus, when you stretch out the double loop, a portion of the string is interlocked, as shown in Illus. 155. Naturally, you don't want spectators to see this interlocked portion. So, as you double the loop, quickly slide your right hand along the doubled string and conceal the interlock.

Move your left hand to within a few inches (cm) of your right, so that you're offering a small length of string for Craig, a helpful spectator, to cut with the scissors (Illus. 156). You very wisely handed Craig the scissors before you started playing with the string.

Invariably, your helper will cut at about the middle of the portion offered.

Illus. 155

Hold up the string in your right hand, demonstrating that it's in two pieces. Making sure you keep the inter-lock concealed with your right fingers, carefully tie the ends of the small piece into a square knot. Now you

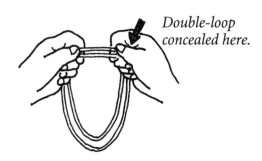

Double-loop concealed here.

Illus. 156

need no longer conceal anything. Ask Craig to hold the two loose ends of the string. Make some mystical waves over the string, mumbling some magic words. Look a little disappointed. Try again. You're even more disappointed. "The magic doesn't seem to be working," you tell Craig. "But I'd like to give you a little something for helping out. I know you won't take money, so what can I give you? I've got it!" Slide the knot along the string, moving his hand to one side as you remove the knot from the string. Present him with the knot. Hold up the string by the ends. "Say! That *is* sort of magic."

And Slide Again

Using (about) a 3' (1 m) piece of string or cord, you might try this trick, which is about as easy as magic ever gets.

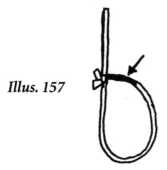

Illus. 157

Hold the string at one end and let it hang down. Ask Donna to point out the middle of the string. Take one end and tie it to the string at that point (Illus.157).

Make sure you keep track of the portion leading to the knot, which is darkened in the illustration. Ask Donna to cut the "middle of the string." Actually have her cut at the point indicated by the arrow in Illus. 157. Do so by holding the string between your hands and presenting only this portion to her.

Ask Donna to hold both ends of the string. You can now slide off the knot and present it to her, as you did in the previous trick. The following, however, might be a better conclusion. Hold the knot in your right fist. Bring your left hand over, apparently to take the knot. Actually, your left hand grips the point where the knot was, while your right hand slides the knot to your right. As you continue sliding the knot to the end of the string, say, "Could you pull the string a little tighter?" Move her hand aside with yours. She regrips the string, and you slide the knot off.

You can casually put your right hand in your pocket and leave the knot there as you massage the string with your left hand, restoring it. Or you can go to your pocket for *magic dust*, leaving the knot there. The invisible *magic dust* is sprinkled over your left hand, bringing about the restoration of the string.

The Incredible Knot

G. W. Hunter invented this clever trick. You can use a 3' (1 m) length of string, cord, or rope.

You ask, "The question is, 'Can anyone tie a knot in a

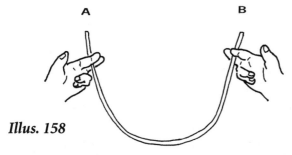

A   B

Illus. 158

string without letting go of the ends?' The answer is no, unless you happen to be magical, a no-good sneak, or a

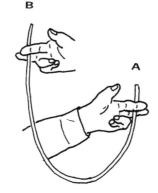

B

A

Illus. 159

lowdown rascal. And since I'm two out of three of those, I'll give it a try. Watch closely as I tie a knot without letting go of the ends."

Hold the string between your hands, as shown (Illus. 158).

For convenience the string is shown as shorter than it actually is.

Bring end B over your left wrist (Illus. 159) and around the back of your left hand to the position shown in Illus. 160. Bring end B through the loop, as shown by the dark arrow in Illus. 160. Do not let go of end B.

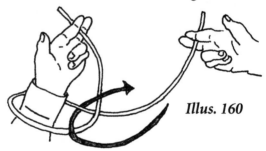

Illus. 160

Say, "I've done nothing underhanded—well, I have done something underhanded and (actually) overhanded—but nothing you haven't seen. The ends haven't left my fingers, yet the knot is already formed. But I do not use sleight of hand; I use magic. To prove it,

I'm not going to do anything fast, or switch the ends, or do anything else sneaky." Address Mike, a spectator, "I want you to take one end in each hand and pull." When he does, a knot will form in the middle of the string.

Knot at All

Here's simple, effective follow-up to the two preceding tricks.

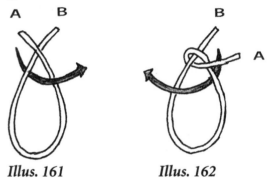

Illus. 161   *Illus. 162*

Invite Martin and Wally to help out. Take the ends of your 3' (1 m) string in your hands, about 5" (13 cm) from the ends. Cross the right-hand section in front of the left (as you look at it) and grip the intersection between your left thumb and fingers. Pull End A through the loop (Illus. 161). Pull End A to the right for several inches (cms) and then hand the end to Martin, asking him to hold that end for a moment.

Transfer the intersecting point (now a knot, but only briefly) to your right hand, so that you're now holding the point between your right thumb and fingers. Put End B through the loop, as indicated by the arrow shown in Illus. 162. Pull End B to the left for several inches, and hand that end to Wally.

Still covering the "knot" with your right hand, ask Martin and Wally to pull on the string. When the string is taut, say, "Whoa! You pulled too hard. The knot popped right off." Remove your right hand from the string and toss the invisible knot into the air. Invite them to examine the string—the knot's gone!

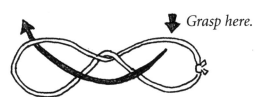

Grasp here.

Illus. 163

Or Knot to Be

Similar in *effect* to the preceding trick, this may well be the easiest method to cause a "knot" to disappear.

Take the ends of a 3' (1 m) string and tie them together. Hold the loop in your hands, as shown in Illus. 152, page 217. Make sure that your right hand covers the knot.

Give the loop one complete twist (Illus. 163).

This, in effect, divides the string into two loops. With your left hand, reach past the point where the string crosses, grasp one of the strands, and pull the strand through the loop on the left. The dark arrow in Illus. 163 shows this process. Pull the ends so that a knot forms in the middle. One of the strands (probably the top one) will slide through the knot. Say, "We'd better tighten the knot." Cover the knot with your left hand and pull on the appropriate strand with your right hand, sliding the knot to the left. When the knot is quite small, grip it tightly between your left thumb and left first finger. Jerk the strand with your right hand, pretending to tighten the knot. Actually, of course, the so-called knot can vanish by simply holding the string on either side of the knot and pulling on the other side. Go to the actual knot and, in similar fashion, tighten it. "Might as well tighten this one, too."

Go back to the false knot and grip it lightly between your left thumb and left first finger; your other fingers grip the string. "I need a lot more fibre in my diet. This could be a start." With your right hand, grasp the same strand it held before and pull the strand tight, popping the knot out of the string. At the same time, with your left hand, apparently pick off the knot and pop it into your mouth. As you chew and swallow, display the string, showing that the knot's gone.

Eye of the Needle

There's no particular relationship between the simplicity of a trick and the audience reaction. Here's a good example. The trick itself is very easy to perform, but the audience is usually astonished. What's more, because the result seems so impossible, you'll be delightfully surprised every time you perform it. To achieve this wonderful result, however, you must follow the instructions carefully.

You'll need a 3' (1 m) length of cord or string. Ask, "Has anyone here ever tried to thread a needle?" After the response, continue, "Well, I find it almost impossible. In fact, the only way I can do it is by resorting to magic. Let me show you what I mean."

Illus. 164

Grasp the string about 8" (20 cm) from the bottom and wrap it around your thumb in a clockwise direction at least a half-dozen times. The string should be wrapped fairly loosely. Form a loop in the string, holding it between your left thumb and your left first finger (Illus. 164).

Display the loop, saying, "This is the eye of the needle." With your right fingers and thumb, grasp the 8" (20 cm) length of string you let hang loose at the beginning. Hold it a few inches (cms) from the end. "This is the thread. You can see that the eye of this particular needle is enormous. Even so, I'll probably have difficulty threading it. But to make it even more difficult, I'll try to thread the needle—without letting go of the thread. Clearly, this calls for magic. So let me try my magic words:

Maybe my outstanding speed'll
Help me push this through the needle.

Now it's time for some great acting. With a quick forward movement, try to push the "thread" through the eye. Failure! Repeat the magic words and try again. Another failure! Again the magic words, and yet another failure. Say the magic words with great emphasis, and you'll finally succeed. Well, not actually. On your last attempt, brush the bottom of the loop with the bottom of your right hand, and then pull the string sharply upwards, letting a loop slip off your left thumb. It indeed looks as though you threaded the needle without letting go of the "thread."

Say, "It worked! So next time you want to thread a needle, try to remember the magic words."

As you'll discover, it takes some experimentation to get the moves exactly right, but the result is well worth the effort.

Candy Is Dandy

This is a trick in which you reveal the "secret" at the end. If you prefer, you could eliminate the last part and do the trick as straight magic.

All you need for this trick is a length of string, a handkerchief, and a roll of multicolored hole-in-the-middle candy.

In your right pocket you have a length of string and a candy, preferably light-colored. In your left pocket, you have a bright-colored candy at the bottom and a folded handkerchief well above it. On top of all this, you have a piece of candy which is the same color as the candy you have in your right pocket.

Reach into your right pocket and take out the candy

Illus. 165

and the string. Hold up the candy for all to see. Run the string through the hole, and then run one end of the string through the hole again so that the candy is held at the bottom of a loose loop (Illus. 165).

This is done as misdirection; spectators might feel that there's something tricky about the way the candy is held on the string.

Get two spectators to hold the ends of the string. Reach into your left pocket. Grip the candy in your loosely curled fingers. Grasp a corner of the handkerchief between your first finger and thumb and pull the cloth from your pocket, snapping it open. Use both hands to lay the handkerchief over the string, concealing the candy that's hanging there.

Take the candy from your left hand into your right. Chat fairly loudly about the difficulty of the feat you're trying to perform; you're trying to cover any noise you might make as you break the candy that's hanging on the string. Make as clean a break as you can, because you don't want to deal with too many little pieces. Hold these pieces in your curled left fingers.

Hold the unbroken candy between your right fingertips and your right thumb. Drop your left hand down so that you can grasp an edge of the handkerchief between your first finger and your thumb. Whip the handkerchief off the string, and, with your right hand, hold up the candy for all to see.

Immediately, place the handkerchief into your left pocket. Shove the pieces of candy to the bottom of your left pocket. Grasp the multicolored candy and rest it on top of the handkerchief. Remove your hand from your pocket.

As you produce the liberated candy, some spectators may see through the trick. Don't let them analyze. Instantly say, "Don't say a word. I know exactly what you're thinking. Can he possibly do that again? Of course I can."

Quickly thread the candy onto the string, exactly as before. Have your assistants hold the ends of the string. Reach into your left pocket and take the bright-colored candy into your curled fingers. Grip the handkerchief between your thumb and your first finger and pull the handkerchief from your pocket. Be careful that you don't bring out any broken candy pieces along with the handkerchief. Proceed exactly as before. The broken pieces go into your left pocket, along with the handkerchief, and the liberated candy is held up for all to see.

There's one little problem: It's a different color! Stare at it for a moment in apparent shock. Say, "Oh-oh!" Pause briefly. Then say, "Real magic, ladies and gentlemen. Not only have I removed the candy from the string, but I've magically caused it to change color."

Join in the general merriment. Sometimes a few of the less astute in your audience will wonder what all the laughter is about.

A Bouncy Band

For this amusing stunt, you'll need two rubber bands.

Say, "Some people tie a piece of string around their finger to remind them of something. I use a rubber band. For example, I was supposed to buy one or two loaves of bread, so I put a rubber band around my first and second fingers." Place one rubber band over the first two fingers of your right hand, displaying it as shown (Illus. 166 — your view). Holding the back of your right hand towards

Illus. 166

Illus. 167

the onlookers, pull back the rubber band, using your left hand. Close the fingers of your right hand, so that when you release with your left hand, the rubber band will be outside all of your fingers (Illus. 167).

"Unfortunately, rubber bands aren't very reliable, so when I go to the store..." Straighten up your right-hand fingers. The rubber band will jump over, so that it will surround the other two fingers. "...the rubber band was on my third and fourth fingers. So I bought four loaves of bread."

Repeat the stunt, saying, "This kept happening to me every time I went to the store."

The feat you're about to perform is actually no more difficult than your first stunt, but it seems to be miraculous. "One day I decided to trap the rubber band so that it couldn't switch fingers on me."

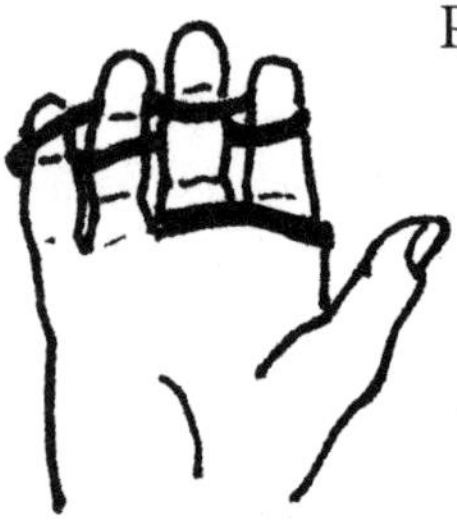

Place the rubber band over the first two fingers of your right hand, as you did before. Pick up the other rubber band with your left hand and wrap it around the fingers of your right hand.

"But when I got to the store..."

Follow the exact same procedure as before, and the rubber band will once again jump over so that it encircles the other two fingers. Shrug.

Illus. 168

"Again, four loaves of bread." Shake your head. "It didn't matter. I was supposed to buy milk anyway."

That Band Really Jumps

It's always fun to involve a spectator in a funny bit of by-play. Ruth is supposed to have a great sense of humor; let's test it.

Place a rubber band on the first finger of your left hand, letting the band hang down (Illus. 169).

Bring the band under your middle finger (Illus. 170), and then over the top of your middle finger. Hook the end of the band onto the tip of your first finger. (Illus. 171) shows a simplified view of the final position. The rubber band should be at the very end of your fingers, attached between the first joint and the tip.

Hold your left hand upright, and ask Ruth to hold the tip of your first finger and end up around your middle finger.

Illus. 169

Illus. 170

Illus. 171

Now it's time to display your performance skills. Stare at the rubber band with a puzzled look. Frown at Ruth. "I thought I asked you to hold my first finger. Let's try again."

Repeat the whole routine, admonishing Ruth," Now would you please hold on?" By the third time, she should really be squeezing the tip of your first finger. You might complain in mock seriousness, "Ow! That's tight enough."

You should probably quit after three or four tries, thanking Ruth for giving it a try. "After all, you did your best. It's probably not all your fault that it didn't work out."

The Hindu Bangle Trick

Effect: From the fabled regions of the Indian subcontinent comes the Hindu Bangle Trick, which, when performed well, is truly amazing. Follow closely the details of its presentation.

Ask someone to come forward from the audience to assist you. Hand him a stout length of rope, about two and a half feet in length, and have him tie both ends of the rope to your wrists (Illus. 172).

The knots should be very tight and even sealed with tape to heighten the effect.

Next, hand your assistant a plastic ring some four inches in diameter. Instruct him to pass it among the audience to verify that it is not a trick ring or has been tampered with in any way. When he returns the ring to you, instruct him to drape a three-foot-square cloth over your hands and arms. Then tell him to step back and slowly count to five, let the cloth slip to the floor; the audience will see that the ring is now threaded on the rope. On examination, your wrists are found to be securely bound (Illus. 173).

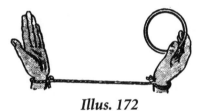

Illus. 172

Illus. 173

Instruct your assistant to cut you free, and step back to acknowledge the thunderous applause.

Materials Needed:
- Two matching bangles
- A three-foot-square cloth

• A stout, two-and-a-half-foot length of rope

Presentation: How is this trick accomplished? When you go to the magic store (Woolworth's of course), buy two matching bangles. When you present this trick, the second one is already on your arm, halfway up your sleeve. Under cover of the cloth, slip your hand up your sleeve and bring the bangle down. Hold this bangle with one hand while slipping the first bangle (the one you showed to the audience) with your other hand onto a hook inside your coat. Or, slip the ring back up the sleeve of your coat and get rid of it as soon as possible.

Here, There, Everywhere

Effect: All that is needed to perform this rope trick is a four-foot length of rope and an eight-inch-diameter wooden embroidery ring. (Any large, solid ring will do.) Pick up a piece of rope and show it to the audience. There are three knots tied in the rope. The solid wooden ring hangs on one of the end knots (Illus. 174).

Pass the rope behind your back, and the ring will jump to the knot at the other end of the rope (Illus. 175). Once again pass the rope behind your back, and the ring jumps back to the other end (Illus. 174). The third time you do this, however, the ring is found to have jumped to the middle knot (Illus. 176).

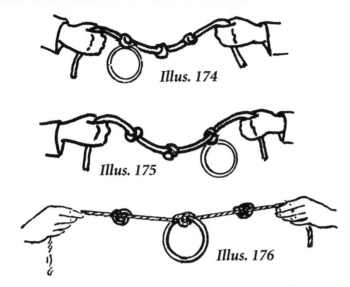

Illus. 174

Illus. 175

Illus. 176

Immediately hand the rope, with the ring still securely tied to the middle knot, out for inspection.

The secret lies in the fact that there is a fourth knot tied in the rope. This knot is hidden by your hand, which covers the knot when you hold the rope (Illus.177). Also, the bottom knot on the rope is a slip knot (Illus. 178).

Presentation: Pick up the rope with your right hand, remembering to conceal the extra knot (Illus. 177) and hold it up to the audience (Illus. 178). When you pass the rope behind your back, cover the end with the extra knot with your left hand. Then show the rope to the

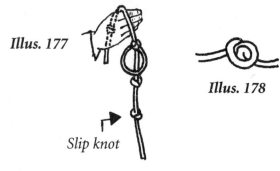

Illus. 177

Illus. 178

Slip knot

audience (Illus. 175). The previous action is reversed for the next pass. During the final pass behind your back, pull the rope tight so that slip knot will come apart and disappear. Now bring the rope out. The ring will be on the middle knot. A perfect deception.

A Knotty Problem

Effect: Stand before the audience and ask: "Did you ever have one of those days where everything seems to go wrong? Of course you have. The other day I was practicing tying some knots while I was working on a new escape trick. First, I tied a reef knot like this one, but when I pulled it tight it just disappeared. See, the same thing has happened with this knot.

"Next, I tried tying a Bulgarian Shoelace Knot, but when I went to pull it tight, it too disappeared just like this.

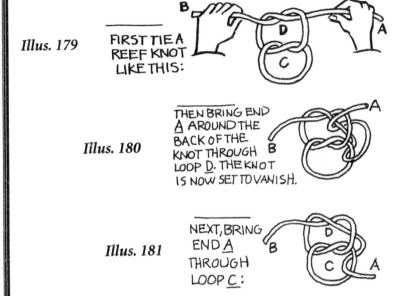

Illus. 179 FIRST TIE A REEF KNOT LIKE THIS:

Illus. 180 THEN BRING END A AROUND THE BACK OF THE KNOT THROUGH LOOP D. THE KNOT IS NOW SET TO VANISH.

Illus. 181 NEXT, BRING END A THROUGH LOOP C:

"Luckily, when I tried to tie a knot without letting go of either end my magic powers returned and I succeeded" (at this point, use the Impossible Knot, pages 243 to 247).

Materials Needed:

• One three-foot length of soft rope

Presentation: Let's start with the first knot to disappear, the Reef Knot. Just follow the instructions in Illus. 179-181. When the knot is made it looks formidable, but it will melt away like butter when you pull the ends apart.

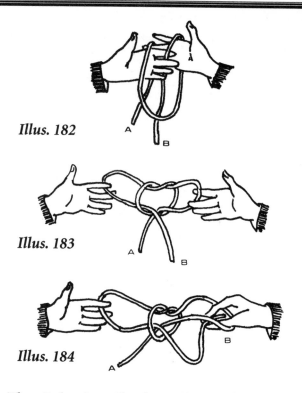

Illus. 182

Illus. 183

Illus. 184

The Bulgarian Shoelace Knot takes a bit more description. Place the rope over your hands as shown in Illus. 182. Clip the two loops between the first and second fingers of each hand and pull your hands apart (Illus. 183). Pull the rope tight and you will have formed a shoelace knot. Next, reach through the right-hand loop with the thumb and first finger of your right hand

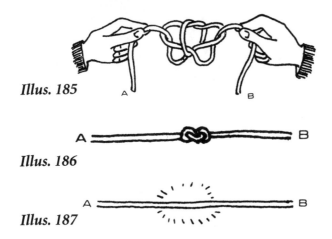

Illus. 185

Illus. 186

Illus. 187

and grasp end B of the rope (Illus. 184).

Do the same with your left hand, grasping end A. Pull the ends through the loops (Illus. 185) and pull the rope tight, forming a knot in the middle (Illus. 186). Pause a moment and then pull hard on the two ends. The knot will disappear in the twinkling of an eye (Illus. 187).

This presentation, in which you have failed to tie two different knots, is a perfect lead-in to the Impossible Knot.

Impossible Knot

Effect: Challenge someone in the audience to come forward and tie a knot in a three-foot length of rope without letting go of either end of the rope. After he has made a few unsuccessful attempts, take the rope from him and proceed to show how it can be done three different ways. This is a trick that violates the axiom of never showing the same trick more than once to the same audience.

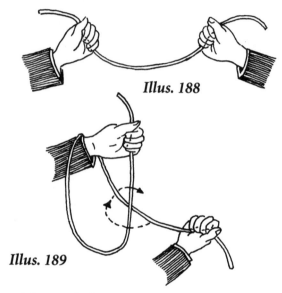

Illus. 188

Illus. 189

Materials Needed:
- A three-foot length of the soft rope
- Transparent tape

Presentation: For the first method of tying, place the rope on a tabletop. Fold your arms in front of your chest and bend over the table. With your left hand, reach under your right arm and pick up the right end of the rope. With your right hand, reach over your left arm and pick up the left end of the rope.

Now, unfold your arms, drawing them apart. Stretch them far apart, and a knot will be formed in the center of the rope. This is method one.

For the second method, pick up the rope in both hands as shown in Illus. 188. Now, loop the rope over and behind your left wrist as shown in Illus. 189.

Continue looping by weaving the end around the back strand as shown in Illus. 189 and 190. When you're finished, your hands, palms up, should look like the hands shown in Illus. 191.

Now comes the important move of the trick. Turn both palms down, letting the loops slide off the back of your hands. However, when you do this your right hand should let go of rope end A and grasp the rope at point C. As the loops slide off your hands, rope end A slides through loop B; this allows you to stretch your arms apart, thus forming a knot in the center of the rope (Illus. 192). The action is so fast that the audience cannot see you releasing and then regrasping the end of the rope.

At this point, pause and pretend to see a look of doubt in one or two faces in the audience. Then say, "I think that one or two of you are still not convinced that

Illus. 190

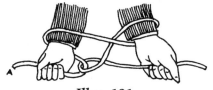

Illus. 191

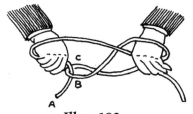

Illus. 192

I can indeed tie a knot in a rope without letting go of either end. Very well, I will show you once again, but this time I will do it under test conditions!"

Now have the gentleman who first assisted you take the transparent tape and firmly tape each end of the rope to your first fingers (Illus. 193).

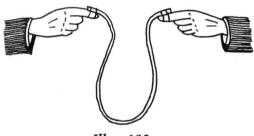

Illus. 193

When this is done, repeat the previous steps up through and including Illus. 191. At this point say, "I have just completed the knot, but you cannot see it. To prove it, I want this gentleman to remove the ends of the rope from my fingers and to then stretch the rope apart. There, you see! There is a knot in the middle just as I said there would be. I've shown you how to do this feat three different ways. Now go home and entertain your friends with this amazing bit of rope magic!"

The Impossible Linking Ropes

Effect: You, the magician, will perform the seemingly impossible task of linking together two pieces of rope while they are hidden under a handkerchief.

Materials Needed:

• Two three-foot lengths of rope. One rope is white, and the other is dyed red.

• One heavy pocket handkerchief.

Presentation: Place the two lengths of rope on the table in front of you. Loop each rope in the form of a U and place them side-by-side as shown in Illus. 194. The loop ends should be towards you.

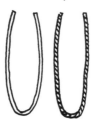

Illus.194

Next, open up a heavy white pocket handkerchief and drape it over the two ropes, leaving the ends exposed (Illus. 195). Now, reach under the handkerchief and tell your audience that you are causing the ropes to link together. What you are doing is to pull one side of the

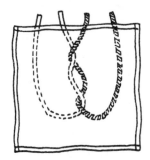

Illus. 195

red rope over the nearer side of the white rope, and then to tuck the red rope back under, as shown in Illus. 195.

A moment later, bring your hands out and take hold of the bottom ends of the handkerchief. Then draw the handkerchief away from you until the linked loops of the rope came into view (Illus. 196). Keep moving the cloth down until the ends of the rope are covered.

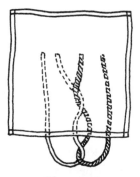

Illus. 196

Move your hands back to the top of the cloth, and then pick up the two linked ropes and the handkerchief as one and hold it up in front of you (Illus. 197). At this point the cords will untangle themselves automatically behind the cloth. After three or four seconds, let the handkerchief drop to the table. Lay the two linked ropes down on the table in front of you and elaborate on the impossibility that the audience has just witnessed.

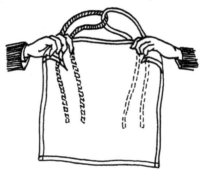

Illus. 197

Perfect Rope Trick

Effect: To the audience, this will seem to be truly an "impossible" rope trick. Display three pieces of rope, all of different lengths. Then cause the shortest piece to grow in length and the longest piece to shrink until all the pieces are of the same length. After showing each

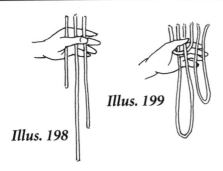

Illus. 198

Illus. 199

piece to the audience, cause the pieces of rope to return to their original lengths. Then immediately pass out the three pieces for examination.

Materials Needed: Three pieces of rope. The short piece should be 12" long, the medium piece 28", and the long piece 42".

Presentation: Hold up the short piece of rope and place it in your left hand. Next, exhibit the long piece and place this in your left hand. Last, show the medium piece and place this too in your left hand (Illus. 198). Keep the back of your left hand turned towards the audience.

Bring the end of the medium-length rope up so that it is next to its other end. Then bring the end of the short piece up and cross it over the end of the long piece that is held in your left hand. Finally, bring the end of the long piece up and over the loop of the short piece (Illus. 199).

Now you are ready to cause all of the ropes to assume the same length. Reach over with your right hand and take hold of one end of the medium-length rope, the end to the right. Also, take hold of the two ends of the long rope. Your left hand is now holding the left end of the medium-length

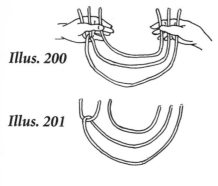

Illus. 200

Illus. 201

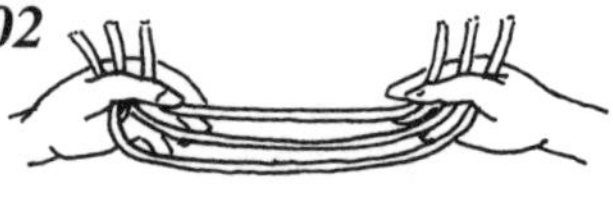

Illus. 202

rope and both ends of the short-length rope. At this point, the short rope and the long rope are looped together. This is hidden from the audience by the back of the left hand.

Grip the ropes tightly with both hands and start to move your hands apart (Illus. 200). Keep moving your hands apart until the ropes appear to be the same length (Illus. 201). Let go of the ends in your right hand. You are now holding the three ropes in your left hand, and they all appear to be of the same length.

At this point, count the ropes, apparently showing each one of them individually. First, reach over and take hold of the medium length of rope and pull it away from your left hand (Illus. 202). Count, "One!"

Then bring your right hand back to get the second rope. What you are actually doing is taking the two ends of the short rope in your right thumb and forefinger and clipping the medium-length rope with the forefinger and index finger of your left hand (Illus. 203). When you move your

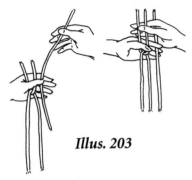

Illus. 203

hands apart, you are holding the looped short and long pieces in your right hand and the medium piece in your left hand (Illus. 204). To the audience it will appear that you placed a second piece of rope into your right hand. Count aloud, "Two!" Through all of this the loop between the two ropes is concealed by both your left and right hands. Both are at all times turned towards the audience.

Finally, move your right hand back and use it to draw the medium-length rope through the fingers of your left hand (Illus. 205). Count aloud, "Three!"

At this point, you have caused the three ropes to become equal in length. To finish the trick, you now have to make them return to their original lengths. Transfer the ropes from your right hand to your left hand (Illus. 206). Make sure that the loop is not seen.

Take the dangling ends of the ropes, one by one,

Illus. 204

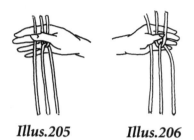

Illus.205 **Illus.206**

and position them in your left hand, as shown in Illus. 207. The ends of each rope should end up being side-by-side in your hand. Now, slowly take hold of one of the ends of the short rope and pull on it until the short rope comes free from your left hand. Make sure that the loop is not drawn up into view. Toss the rope to the audience. Next, draw the medium-length rope from your hand and toss it to the audience. Finally, display the long rope and pass it out for examination.

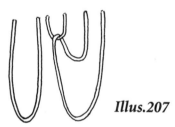

Illus.207

Thus ends the perfect rope trick. There are no "extra" pieces to dispose of; the ropes are genuine, and everything can be examined once the trick is concluded.

Index